From Camel to Truck

FROM CAMEL TO TRUCK

The Bedouin in the Modern World

DAWN CHATTY

First published 1986 by Vantage Press

Revised second edition published 2013 by
The White Horse Press, 10 High Street, Knapwell, Cambridge, CB23 4NR, UK

Set in 11 point Adobe Garamond Pro
Printed by Lightning Source

British Library Cataloguing in Publication Data
A catalogue record for this book is available from the British Library

ISBN 978-1-874267-72-0

For AQ

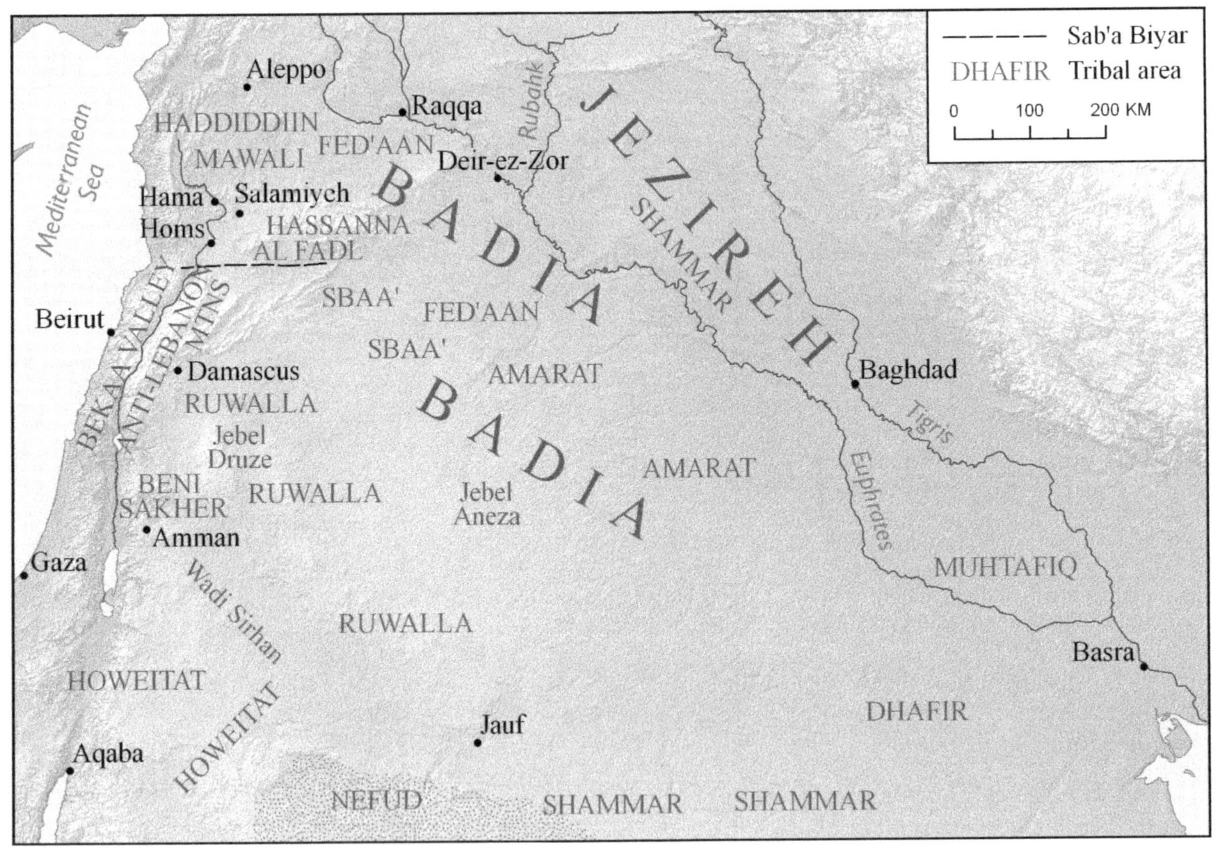

Map 1. The *Badia*

Contents

List of Maps viii

List of Figures and Charts ix

List of Plates x

Acknowledgements xii

Notes on Transliteration of Arabic Words xiii

Foreword to the New Edition 1

Introduction 17

Chapter 1. The Bedouin and How They Came to Be Where They Are 28

Chapter 2. Pacification of the Bedouin in Northern Arabia 44

Chapter 3. Arab Society and the Bedouin 61

Chapter 4. The Camel: The Traditional Way of Life of a Bedouin Household 90

Chapter 5. The Truck: The Changing Pastoral Way of Life 118

Chapter 6. Conclusion: The Bedouin in the Modern World 140

Appendix A: Glossary 155

Appendix B: Table of Measures 158

Selected Bibliography 159

List of Maps

Map 1. The *Badia*. vi

Map 2. Geographical units and marginal zone .29

Map 3. Sykes-Picot Allotment 49

Map 4. Bedouin tribes of Northern Arabia. 72

Map 5. Migration routes of Al-Hassanna and Al-Fadl tribes. 116

Map 6. *Hema* cooperatives and tribal areas 145

List of Figures and Charts

FIGURES

Figure 1. Aneza confederation of tribes. 39

Figure 2. Descent line of Sheikh Tamir-il-Milhem 80

Figure 3. Descent line of Emir Mit'ib Sha'laan 81

Figure 4. Descent line of Emir Faour 83

Figure 5. Genealogical tree of Beit Saalih 95

Figure 6. Daily activities of men. 111

Figure 7. Daily activities of women 112

CHARTS

Chart 1. Income and expenditure, household of 5–8 persons with a herd of 134 sheep, 1960s. 115

Chart 2. Income of average household of 5–8 persons with a herd of 134 sheep, 1963 and 1973. 128

Chart 3. Sheep marketing. 131

Chart 4. One week in late summer (1973) selected in order to illustrate the range of commercial activities in which the truck is used. 137

List of Plates

Plate 1. Camels going out to pasture in the Syrian desert (Al-Fed'aan) . 17

Plate 2. Young men riding camels out to pasture (Al-Fed'aan) in the Syrian desert 23

Plate 3. Family in front of tent in the Syrian desert (Al-Fed'aan) 25

Plate 4. Close-up of male guests eating at a wedding (Al-Fadl) 63

Plate 5. A wedding celebration in Bekka Valley of Lebanon (Al-Fadl) 65

Plate 6. Male guests at wedding (Al-Fadl) 66

Plate 7. Woman milking sheep (Al-Hassanna) 68

Plate 8. Man pouring coffee for guests (Al-Hassanna). 71

Plate 9. Summer tent (Al-Hassanna) in the Bekaa Valley of Lebanon . . 91

Plate 10. Abu Ali (Al-Fadl) 93

Plate 11. Woman mending tent flap in the Syrian desert (Al-Fed'aan) 94

Plate 12. Young woman baking bread (Al-Fed'aan). 97

Plate 13. Young woman dressed for a wedding (Al-Fadl). 99

Plate 14. Young mother and child (Al-Hassana) 105

Plate 15. Mother with young children (Al-Fadl) 108

Plate 16. Mother and daughter: the modern and the traditional (Al-Fadl) 109

Plate 17. Mother and child (Al-Fed'aan). 113

Plate 18. Two young women and child (Al-Fed'aan). 115

Plate 19. Truck being packed for a move to new pasture land in the Syrian desert (Al-Fed'aan) 118

Plate 20. Family climbing aboard a fully packed truck in the Syrian desert (Al-Fed'aan) 119

Plate 21. Children and grandmother enjoying breakfast cup of tea and bread (Al-Fed'aan). 122

Plate 22. Young mother preparing tea on kerosene stove (Al-Fed'aan). 124

Plate 23. Young woman in 'kitchen' of tent (Al-Fed'aan) 125

Plate 24. Visitors from another tribe relaxing in guest section of an Al-Fed'aan tent 129

Plate 25. Author with young mother and children (Al-Fed'aan) 141

Acknowledgments

It is not possible to express my appreciation and gratitude adequately to all those teachers, colleagues, friends, and relatives who gave me the encouragement and opportunity to undertake the research that went into the preparation of this book. Nevertheless, I wish to acknowledge my indebtedness to three individuals: my graduate teacher, Professor Hilda Kuper, whose support and training prepared me for field research; my father, Dr. Dia E. Chatty, whose cooperation and timely assistance greatly facilitated the process of data collection and analysis; and finally my husband, Oliver Nicholas Patrick Mylne, without whose patience and strength this book could never have been completed. I dedicate this work to them.

ACKNOWLEDGMENTS FOR THE NEW EDITION

I would very much like to thank Sarah Johnson for her support and encouragement to prepare a new edition of this book. It had been on my mind for some time but I had not found the empathetic editor this work required until I met Sarah. I would also like to thank Michael Atherton at the Bodleian Library who redrew the maps, using advances in digital cartography to give greater accuracy and clarity to original drawings.

Notes on the Transliteration of Arabic Words

Arabic terms have been for the most part transliterated upon recognized lines. All Arabic words in the text are italicized unless they are relatively common in English usage (e.g., caliph, sheikh, emir). The first time an Arabic term appears in the text the English equivalent is given in parenthesis, if its meaning is not apparent otherwise. Thereafter the reader must refer to the first mention in text or preferably to the glossary.

Foreword

In March of 1973, I sat in the sumptuous, chandelier-lit reception room of the Emir Faour of the Fadl Bedouin tribe awaiting an interview. I had visited this elegant apartment in the Corniche district of Beirut a number of times over the past six months hoping to secure permission to begin ethnographic fieldwork with an extended family of the Fadl tribe, which moved between Syria and Lebanon. I had identified this tribe the year before in the University of California Social Science Library in Los Angeles. It was the 'perfect' field site to test my doctoral dissertation hypothesis. I wanted to challenge the ontological assumptions common in the literature at that time indicating that pastoralists were irrational, backward and resistant to change. I wanted to test my own theory that pastoralists did not resist change which they saw in their own interests; that they did indeed make rational economic decisions. To that end, I had identified a Ph.D. dissertation conducted by the son of the Emir of this tribe, Sheikh Fadl, undertaken nearly ten years earlier (1964) and supervised by the eminent social anthropologist Raymond Firth, a professor at the London School of Economics. I felt that, with this earlier study as a base line, I would indeed be able to determine the extent, if any, of economic rationality, entrepreneurship and development in the tribe.

I had arrived in Beirut in October 1972 hoping to get out into 'the field' by January 1973. I had registered my interest in doing some part-time teaching at the American University of Beirut (AUB) and then proceeded to try to find the Fadl tribe. Everyone I talked to insisted there were no Bedouin in Lebanon. I persisted in my search, giving a number of talks on the subject at AUB, at the British Council and the American Cultural Centre. Finally a staff member of the British Council approached me and told me that she had been out in the central Bekaa Valley and had identified a relative, a landowner in the town of Kab Elias, just over the mountains who had good relations with the Emir Tamir el Milhelm of another Bedouin tribe, the Hassanna. That was encouraging news.

At about the same time I made another contact, someone who actually knew the son of the Emir of the Fadl. A meeting was set up but then cancelled at the last minute. Several months went by with meetings agreed, dates changed, postponed again and then cancelled. Eventually a close cousin in Damascus realized that she knew Sheikh Fadl's sister and she too began to help me pursue a meeting with him. Then in the depth of winter a meeting did take place with the elusive Sheikh. We discussed my plans to do a follow up study to test the hypothesis of economic rationality and growth. Sheikh Fadl liked the idea and promised to arrange a meeting with his father to gain his approval.

Another round of waiting ensued, punctuated by postponed, delayed and cancelled meetings. Although I used the time as efficiently as I could, the tension and the worry as months passed that this contact was not going to work out were oppressive. Finally, Sheikh Fadl confided in me that his father had agreed to allow me to study the tribe but only on condition that my father gave his consent. That consent would have to be given verbally in a face-to-face meeting. I was dumbstruck. Having spent the last decade as an independent minor and then adult university student in California I had somehow convinced myself that I was a liberated young woman. Yet now, come what may, I was not going to be able to progress my fieldwork without intervention from my father. A phone call to Mogadishu, Somalia, where my father was completing his appointment as the WHO Resident Representative, went well. Of course he would travel to Beirut and meet with the Emir of the Fadl. It was his duty and his pleasure.

My father sat next to me on the sofa in the Emir's reception room. We were kept waiting only long enough to be served cups of dark, bitter cardamom infused coffee. As we finished this traditional Bedouin drink, the Emir Faour and his son, Sheikh Fadl, joined us. My father and the Emir engaged in a few minutes of light conversation, establishing their relationship to several circles of acquaintances and colleagues in Lebanon and Syria. Eventually the subject turned to my proposed field study and my wish to be placed with an extended family of Fadl Bedouin in Lebanon. The Emir agreed to take me out into the field and return me to my father safe and unharmed. The journey would take place the following day.

The next morning I was shown to a seat in the back of the Emir's Cadillac alongside the Emir; in the front seats were the chauffer and another of the Emir's sons. I have no recollection of our conversation during this journey; but I do remember that I noticed that every man in the car wore a large, jewel-encrusted watch, each set to a different time or time zone. The drive from Beirut to the field site was just under two hours. We arrived at a settlement of tents and stone buildings along the foot of the Anti-Lebanon Mountains. The entourage had been expected; it was a day of celebration. The Emir's visits were infrequent, so this was a very special occasion. I believe he had other business than mine to discuss, but I was whisked away by the women of the extended family group and hosted in another compound for a short while. As the Emir prepared to leave, I was summoned to the *majlis* (reception area) where he sat with the elders of the tribal lineage. 'Abu Ali', he said to the family head, 'She is to be returned to me when she has finished her work, with not a hair on her head touched'. And with that he got up and left. My book *From Camel to Truck* had been conceived.

Nearly 35 years later I returned to this same settlement. It was 2006 and I was conducting a study of Bedouin health care in the region and I wanted to see how the Bedouin in Lebanon had fared. It had changed little except that the tents had disappeared and been replaced with small cement block units, some of two rooms, others three. I identified a few of the adults I had known; Abu Ali's daughter-in-law and her children still lived in the house I had sat in many an hour. A few of the young women I had known in the 1970s were still there. I had attended a number of their weddings. But their husbands had all died in their fifties. Health care was problematic as, for most of them, citizenship had not been forthcoming, despite constant lobbying in the intervening decades, and thus they had no access to government health services. When I had researched my book, I had been pleased to find that a policy of 'benign neglect' characterized state–tribal interaction. A move had been underway to petition the state to grant this group of Bedouin citizenship. The Emir Faour was involved in these negotiations. At the time I had thought that being ignored and left alone by the state was better than being forced to settle. What I had not considered was that three decades later they would still not have been recognized as citizens; the long-term impact of such marginalization was clearly expressed in terms of poor health care.

The lack of citizenship remains a serious issue in Lebanon but not in Syria or the other Arab states where Bedouin are found. The peculiar consociational political system set into place in Lebanon by the French during their Inter War Mandate meant that a balance had to be maintained between Muslim and Christians. Many Bedouin held centuries old grazing rights in the Bekaa Valley. They, and their leader, had refused to register with the French National Census Authority in 1932, believing it to be a colonial rule rather than an independent nation-state. In addition, the French Authorities did not wish to add Sunni Muslim numbers – the Bedouin are by and large all Sunni Muslim – to the official population figures which would have tilted towards a Muslim majority (Maktabi 1999). The Bedouin in Lebanon are still paying the price for that decision, with either no nationality papers or papers stating that their 'citizenship' is *qayd il-dars* (under study). Of nearly 150,000 Bedouin in Lebanon only 40–60,000 hold nationality papers and have the right to vote (Chatty 2010b). Those with voting rights are now being courted by political parties determined to swing the balance of Muslims in the country from a Shiite to a Sunni majority.

In Syria my contact with the Bedouin had been more continuous over the years. I worked with and for a number of Bedouin tribes in the country in various capacities related to rural development. I had observed numerous Bedouin celebrations and interactions with non-Bedouin and I had come to know well the Emirs of the Ruwalla Bedouin visiting them frequently at their *majlis*, Beit Sha'laan, in Damascus. Over the decades I had studied the variable economic successes of some Bedouin families as well as the impoverishment of others (Chatty 1996a). Here, at least, the government policy of benign neglect had allowed some Bedouin to expand their horizons and to benefit from transnational relations and trade particularly with Saudi Arabia. Slowly, I had come to reaffirm the importance of hospitality as a Bedouin institution and a mechanism for maintaining and promoting the authority of lineage and tribal leadership. The latter was vested in a moral authority which could be augmented or lost by behaviour that either respected or disregarded family norms and custom, particularly with regard to the practice of hospitality. *Karam*, the Arabic term which can be translated as hospitality or generosity, was ultimately also about security, protection and respect. By the late twentieth century, a resurgence of tribal political strength was becoming obvious in Syria. Government efforts to snuff out tribal leadership roles in party politics seem to have backfired and instead a growth in Bedouin representation in Parliament was clearly evident (Chatty 2010c). More parliamentarians and other officials reaching high rank in the Bath party are self-identifying as Bedouin than has been the case in the past. But who exactly is a Bedouin today?

The past thirty years have seen not only a resurgence of interest in Bedouin tribes, but a confusion of concepts which originated in the neo-colonial efforts during the Inter-War years to settle the moving tribes – the

Bedouin nomadic pastoralists. The British and French authorities prioritized nomadism as the defining feature of these groups' identity. So when some Bedouin were successfully settled – and many have been settled in each of the countries of the Middle East – confusion set in as to what to call them. Were former nomads still Bedouin? Had settlement turned them into farmers? For many state authorities there was a 'wishful thinking' that settled nomads were no longer Bedouin, hence no longer trouble makers who lived at the margins of central authority as in the past. Many of the independent nation states of the region effected legislation in the 1950s and 1960s delegitimising any rights of Bedouin as a social group (e.g. Syria in 1958).

Throughout most of the last century in the Middle East, the term *Bedouin* has been used to describe the nomadic pastoralists of the region. So when herding livestock on natural graze is no longer the main source of livelihood, the previous neo-colonial and early independent nation-state typologies of fully nomadic, semi -nomadic, semi-settled and settled pastoralist become unhelpful. The term is itself derived from the Arabic *bedu,* meaning one who lives in the *Badia* [the semi-arid and arid steppe of Northern Arabia]. In large measure, the term has been used descriptively throughout the regional to differentiate between those peoples whose livelihood is based upon the raising of livestock by mainly natural graze and browse and those who have an agricultural or urban base (*hadar*).

The *bedu–hadar* dichotomy is specific to Arab historiography and has cultural meanings and connotations far beyond the remit of this book. For some, it signifies the opposition of 'civilisation' and the 'lack' of it; for others it is more literally recognized as a distinction between urban and rural life. Still others maintain that the term *bedu* defines a particular cultural group or 'ethnicity' which traces its roots back millennia to the southern edge of the arid Syrian steppe. By 850 BC archaeological evidence reveals a complex of oasis settlements and pastoral camps established by a people known as *arab*. These people were the cultural forerunners of the modern-day Arabs and hence Arab *Bedouin*. The rise of the powerful Islamic Empire in western Arabia in the middle of the seventh century AD gave a dramatic impetus to Arab expansion. As a result the *bedu / hadar* distinction was reproduced in those Arabized territories where such a regional division of labour was ecologically and geographically practicable. The term *Bedouin* also spread, with this expansion resulting in a dual use terminology – one describing a way of life and the other a distinct community, or confederation of tribes.

In my own writing I have preferred to use the term *Bedouin* to describe members of the confederation of tribes of Arabia but I have also in some circumstances used it in its narrower sense as a description of a pastoral lifestyle in the deserts of the Middle East.

Moving beyond this straight forward dichotomous suggestion of meanings, a number of researchers working with Bedouin have begun to ask, just who are they and where have they gone? Although the questions seem simple the answers are not. In the contemporary Middle East, governments do not regard Bedouin as either an 'ethnic' group for inclusion in national census; nor are they identified as a specific occupational group on national identity cards or passports. In spite of this current official and, apparently, international blindness or lack of interest, it is important to grasp the multiplicity of terms and meanings in scientific and popular literature attached to being Bedouin and Bedouin-ness.

For decades policy makers, as well as academic and popular writers have regarded Bedouin and Bedouin-ness as the same as nomadic pastoralists. Some academic books continue to conflate Bedouin with nomad perhaps in order to appeal to a wider audience (see Mundy and Musallam 2000). Government efforts to control these people and to bring them into the orbit of the authority of the state have generally meant settling Bedouin, or turning the nomad into a settled farmer. While all pastoral nomads in the Middle East are Bedouin, the reverse is not necessarily the case.

One prominent anthropologist with rich field experience in Morocco and Oman views the term as generally referring to tribal collectives who 'occupy a place in the social and moral imaginations of the Middle Easterner far beyond their numbers' (Eickelman 1998:39). He sees being 'bedouin' as not necessarily coterminous with nomadic pastoralism, though it may subsume such socio-economic organisation. This approach then encompasses the self-definition and self-identification of many Bedouin who have settled and no longer herd livestock. (Eickelman 1989:74). Recent archaeological evidence in the region is emerging to suggest that Bedouin have moved back and forth between mobile livestock herding and farming in centuries (Lancaster and Lancaster 1995). Another anthropologist with decades of field work in Saudi Arabia sees the Bedouin in recent years as having have been 'exoticized as nomads and essentialized as representatives of segmentary lineage organization and tribalism' for the sake of eco-tourism and other opportunistic activities (Cole 2003:235; Bocco and Chatelard 2001).

Foreword

The association of Bedouin with nomad, shorthand for nomadic pastoralist, remains problematic even today; many Bedouin see themselves as livestock herders, but do not consider themselves nomadic pastoralist. Arabs themselves use the term *bedu ruhhal*, which means migratory or travelling Bedouin to distinguish between Bedouin who move with their herds and those who do not. Bedouin also refer generally to themselves with pride as *Arab*, the term Bedouin applied by others in reference or as a direct form of address is generally regarded as disparaging or an insult (cf Eickelman 1998:40). In Lebanon few Bedouin are migratory; most have settled and live in stone buildings or tin-covered shacks. Some keep small herds locally or with kin who migrate. Further, most have taken up livelihoods in transport, trade and agriculture. It is hardly surprising that in Lebanon, where the drive to be seen as modern and as part of the political landscape is paramount, the term Bedouin or *Bedu* is totally rejected by the Bedouin themselves, in favour of the term *ashairi* (tribal). In Syria, however, where Bedouin all hold nationality papers and continue to practice both long and short-distance migration, the terms *bedu*, *bedu ruhhal*, and *Arab* are commonly used by those who self-identify as Bedouin. When asked directly which term was preferred when making reference to themselves, the Emir of the Ruwalla – who has multiple luxury dwellings in Geneva, Beirut, Damascus and Riyadh – told me, 'We are *bedu ruhhal*, we have large migratory herds and we are proud of that; the *arab* in this country are poor Bedouin who work seasonally in agriculture'. This statement is a carefully constructed reminder that the internal Bedouin hierarchy between 'noble' formerly camel herding tribes and 'common' sheep herding tribes still holds.

The term Bedouin is replete with nuanced critics and prejudices. We have a set of terms; all interrelated, and often used interchangeably, some with greater or lesser accretions of nineteenth century Romanticism and twentieth century Orientalism attached to them. We have the term 'nomadism' which is a geographical term relating to the way space is used; we have the term pastoralism which refers to a livelihood, the raising of livestock by natural graze or pasture; there is also the term tribe *qabila* or *ashira*, a form of social organisation based on kinship – lineages which are segmented for associations of solidarity and power reflected in the Arab proverb 'I against my brother; I and my brother against my cousins; I , my brother and my cousins against the world'; and finally the term Bedouin is a form of cultural identity or ethnicity which I adopt in my work and in this book.

The Bedouin today continue to adapt and change to make the best of the opportunities that surround them. The changes they are adopting are neither simple nor unidirectional. Rather they are complex, with traditions being created and transformed and various notions of modernity also interplaying in this process. Their 'respect and adherence to a range of traditions that help them define and perpetuate their ethnic integrity, their Bedouin-ness' is taking place as they respond to and accommodate significant political, social and economic forces (Khalaf 1990:241). The Bedouin have become many things to many people. The once powerful tribes – based on segmentary lineage structures – have now largely disappeared, but the people remain united by strong kin ties to charismatic leaders who have maintained a moral rather than an economic power base.

In Syria, for example, many of the tribal leaders of the Aneza and Shammar Confederation have strong followings; many maintain websites and post their political positions with regard to their opposition to and support for the current regime on line (Chatty, forthcoming). Lower levels of authority among the tribe continue in some places to be important for managing access to natural resources (Rae 1999; Triulzi 2001). The oil industry and wage paid employment have had significant impacts on economic organisation (Chatty 1996b) and Bedouin have moved into a number of occupations either related to their livestock-raising specialisation or have found, on the fringe of their world, oil company contracts, livestock merchants, transport industry, military service, eco- and commercial tourism, to name a few. The commercialization of Bedouin culture, both for 'eco-tourism' and general tourism, is a growing area of research interest (Cole and Altorki 1998; Dinero 2002; Hazbun 2001).

The individual Bedouin of today is found in many locations. Partially as a result of the 'detribalisation' policies of many of the states of the Middle East in the second half of the twentieth century, the political glue holding Bedouin together in tight kin-based groups has largely dissolved. Some no longer recognize the multiple segments that characterise their 'tribe' but most attach themselves to the figure of tribal leader (Sheikh or Emir). In Lebanon and in Syria, for example, Hassanna Bedouin recognise that their leader is from the family of Milhem. They will say, 'We belong to Milhem'. This belonging is based on the charisma of the person and his adherence to moral principles expressed as 'generosity' and 'hospitality' (Chatty, forthcoming; Schoel 2012) Furthermore, in the region as a whole, when Bedouin who do not know each other meet, they usually ask about each other's lineage, or tribe. Knowing this kin affiliation allows them to place each other in a framework that is meaningful to each other. Kinship, livelihoods, language and cultural markers, traditions and customs all play a part in being Bedouin. Whether that identity is regarded as being tribal or ethnic is an academic debate that is being carried out in competing corridors of academia; Africanists disapprove of the term 'tribal' and its connotations of colonialism; Orientalists hardly recognize the distinction.

The *bidoon* ('without'), a category of peoples which came into prominence after the First Gulf War in the 1990s, is also the subject of some study but should not be confused with Bedouin. The *bidoon* are people 'without' documents [citizenship]. Some *Bedouin* are *bidoon* – that is, they do not hold any state citizenship. In Lebanon, many of the Bedouin remain 'stateless' and are known by the local term *maqtoumeen* (silenced); others have papers indicating that their nationality is *qayd il-dars* (under study). Less than half the Bedouin in Lebanon actually hold full citizenship; these are the descendants of Bedouin who agreed to register in the first [and last] Lebanese census conducted in 1932 during the French Mandate. In Kuwait after the 1990 invasion of the country of Iraq and its aftermath, it emerged that a number of Bedouin groups, who had fled the oil fires near their traditional grazing lands, were prevented from returning to Kuwait as they had no papers. They were descendants of Bedouin who had refused to register in the British sponsored Kuwaiti census of 1921 – being suspicious of British purposes – and hence were not eligible for citizenship. Until the Gulf War this was not problematic, since their widely-ranging movements in the desert steppe were tolerated. But with the security concerns post-1990–1, they found that they were not allowed to return to their usual habitat in Kuwait from their distant traditional grazing lands.

In all parts of the Middle East migratory or mobile Bedouin societies are still found in the arid steppe regions and along the margins of rain-fed cultivation herding livestock. Bedouin living in such areas tend to move their livestock as dictated by the availability of pasture and sometimes seasonal heavy morning dew (occult precipitation). Often they have access to date gardens or they plant grain along their migration routes which they harvest on their return to winter villages or camping areas (Chatty 1986; Cole 1975; Hobbs 1989; Lancaster 1981).

Change and adaptation are key aspects of Bedouin livelihood strategies. This is the fundamental 'fact' I tried to make explicit in this book. Adaptation, opportunism and resilience are the basic elements of contemporary Bedouin life. In the current global economy, many Bedouin have sought out multi-resource strategies, seeking paid employment in related activities such as transport and commerce, entering into the unskilled daily wage labour market in construction and agriculture (Chatty 1996b; Cole and Altorki 1998). Some have commercialized aspects of their culture in order to buy into the growing demand for native trinkets in the expanding eco-tourism market in the Middle East and North Africa (Chatelard 2003; Cole and Altorki 1998; Dinero 2002; Fabian 1983; Loftsdottir 2002). Others have settled and become less mobile. However, regardless of their multiple occupations and residence patterns, they consider themselves Bedouin culturally as long as they maintain close social ties with pastoral kin and retain the local linguistic and cultural markers that identify them as Bedouin.

Over the past nearly 30 years, since the first edition of this book appeared, trucks and other motor vehicles have become an integral part of Bedouin livelihood activity in all parts of the region. Today, the truck is often used to bring feed and water to the herds in the desert as well as to transport goods from one market to another transnationally. Furthermore, the truck has allowed the Bedouin herders to be more mobile than in the past, permitting most to settle for much of the year in permanent villages (especially the young and the old), while still maintaining access to water, pastures, herds and places of employment beyond the arid steppe land that is their home (Cole and Altorki 1998; Lancaster and Lancaster 1999). The mobility and speed of movement which the truck allows has also meant that those with vehicles and large herds can supervise herds and manage a number of related activities using modern information technology (satellite phones, Global Positioning Systems and SMS messaging).

Throughout much of the nineteenth and the first half of the twentieth century the Bedouin, organized themselves in distinct, physically visible segmentary lineage groups and competed with each other at a tribal level for control over sufficient pasture land and water for their herds and their kin. Great battles and frequent skirmishes were recorded by Western explorers and travel writers as the tribes struggled to lay claim to the most fertile parts of the semi-arid and arid lands of the region (Bell 1907; Boucheman 1934; Burkhart 1822; Doughty 1888). By the middle of the twentieth century the policies and actions of the colonial and nation-state era had largely stripped the tribes of their political function. Most governments then set about a concerted policy of 'detribalization and sedentarization' (Fabietti 2000). This was at its height in the Nasserite period of the 1950s and 1960s. However the failure of many international and national schemes to transform Bedouin pastoralists into farmers and to strip their leadership of recognized authority led to a period of 'neglect' in the 1970s and 1980s. The last few decades however have seen a resurgence of Bedouin solidarity and, in some cases, renewed recognition of the authority of its leadership (Chatty 2010a). Some scholars have asked, 'Where have the Bedouin gone?' The answer might be 'Nowhere; we just haven't been looking for them'.

Today, smaller, often lineage-based Bedouin groups seek to manage a land area that contains sufficient resources to sustain communal life. They seek to establish a definite zone of control with well-understood, though often variable, limits and rights of use denied to other Bedouin groups. Among Bedouin these various zones of use-rights or 'ownership' are respected amongst each other. However, most governments throughout the Middle East and North Africa ceased to recognize Bedouin collective territory and largely consider these arid steppe areas 'state-owned' lands. In the past most conflicts were among and between Bedouin tribal groups and generally revolved around the right to use scarce pastures and water resources. The modern nation-state generally tries to settle such conflicts related to land use in government courts relying on the expert advice of respected Bedouin tribal elders (Rae 1999). In Syria, a resurgence of Bedouin authority in the desert (*Badia*) has seen a rise in customary law (*urf*) being used to settle conflict and to arbitrate tribal disputes outside of the government court system (Chatty 2010a).

Most contemporary conflict between the state and Bedouin society focuses on two related areas of concern: the degradation of the arid steppe land and the global interest in preserving the world's biodiversity. For decades, governments in the region have encouraged the Bedouin to move off the arid steppe land and settle. This policy is couched in terms of the 'damage' which Bedouin do to their environment and is derived from theories of land use (equilibrium) which are, according to recent range ecology theory, inappropriate to the dry lands of the Middle East and North Africa (Ellis 1995). Hardin's 1968 publication of his 'tragedy of the commons theory' added little empirical evidence but was widely accepted by governments in the region as further grounds to push the Bedouin to give up their nomadic way of life, which was regarded as destructive of the environment and out of step with modern, settled society (Chatty 1996b).

Academic criticism of the land-use paradigm which has sought to blame the Bedouin for land degradation and desertification is perhaps the most significant development in the age-old struggle for control of the semi-arid and arid steppe land of the traditional Bedouin tribes. This widespread international and national positioning has been used to justify the eviction or severe restriction of Bedouin from their traditional grazing areas. The work of Bocco interrogated the political, administrative and economic roots of this position among international agencies and nation states (1993). This thinking has paved the way for important scholarship questioning government claims of widespread desertification and range degradation due to Bedouin overgrazing and other pastoral activities. As we enter the twenty-first century, indigenous knowledge has come to be recognized as important and the forced assimilation of marginal, minorities no longer fashionable. The work of Debaine and Jaubert in Syria (2002) is one example of efforts to re-examine and largely absolve the Bedouin from the long-standing accusations of causing land degradation by their pastoral practices.

Conservation or the protection of the world's biodiversity also impinges on Bedouin society as, in many parts of the region, important grazing areas or Bedouin grazing reserves for their livestock are being taken over by the state in order to set up nature reserves or to reintroduce endangered mammalian species (e.g. oryx and gazelle). Such projects in Jordan, Israel, Syria, Saudi Arabia and Oman prioritize the needs of those reintroduced or endangered animals over the livelihoods of the local nomadic pastoralists and their herds (Chatelard 2003; Chatty 1998; Spalton *et al.* 1999). The loss of these lands and the failure of many conservation organisations to recognize the traditional knowledge and sustainable practices of the Bedouin represent a further blow to their current livelihood strategies (Chatty and Jaubert 2002). Recent efforts to bring together thinking about biodiversity conservation and nomadic pastoralists have resulted in a growing corpus of studies and advocacy efforts to recognize the contribution which nomadic pastoralists make as guardians of their own traditional territory (Chatty and Colchester 2002). Campaigns by advocates and nomadic pastoralists and other mobile peoples themselves at international fora (e.g. World Parks Congress [WCPA] in 2003 Durban, South Africa and World Conservation

Congresses [IUCN] in Bangkok in November 2004 and Barcelona in 2008) have resulted in recommendations and resolutions protecting the rights of mobile [nomadic] peoples to their lands, advocating their greater integration in biodiversity conservation, and the restitution of their land rights and restoration of their mobility where it has been lost.

CONCLUSION

In the 35 years since I began this research, much has changed. Modern technology has made life more comfortable. Cars, especially four-wheel drive vehicles and large lorries, have given the Bedouin the means to broaden their horizons and their movements. Some have become more mobile, with permanent villages often the abode of the young and the old for much of the year; but spring and summer seeing a refocus on herding livestock to natural gazing areas, relying increasingly on hired shepherds while household heads engage in related trade and transport activities near and far. Some Bedouin have settled and generally given up herding, as is the case for many in Lebanon's Bekaa Valley where the pressure of agricultural expansion made even subsistence herding difficult.

The pressure to settle, to become less nomadic, as a result of government pacification campaigns, rural land reform and confiscation, eviction and exclusion from traditional gazing lands for biodiversity conservation has been led by state authorities and endorsed by many international development organisations. In the long term these activities have undermined the mid-level political organisation of most Bedouin tribes. Lineage leaders who once determined migration routes have become ineffectual, their negotiating services no longer respected or required. This is clearly the case in Lebanon, where only the minority of Bedouin continue to move with their herds. However the powerful political authority and capital of the Bedouin tribal leaders has persisted, despite the decades of under-recognition or outright rejection.

Yet for all the political change, technological innovation and expansion of livelihood practices, Bedouin society remains a coherent kin-based community of social groups attached to segmentary lineages. Their leadership continues to exert a powerful moral authority which these marginalized people respect and to which they respond. The chapters that follow make this abundantly clear. The Bedouin economy is a rational, opportunistic one based on subsistence herding but also one which has widely diversified into related rural enterprises and transnational entrepreneurship. Bedouin society, however, is held together by glue based on the *karam* (hospitality and generosity) of its leading sheikhly family. Nowhere is this more clearly illustrated than in Lebanon, Syria and Saudi Arabia where, for example, the Hassanna tribal leadership in the Milhem family continues to be widely admired and respected.

REFERENCES

Bell, Gertrude. 1907. *Syria, the Desert and the Sown.* London: W. Herman.

Bocco, Riccardo, Ronald Jaubert and Françoise Métral, eds. 1993. *Steppes d'Arabies, états, pasteurs, agriculteurs et commerçants: Le devenir des zones sèches*. Paris: Presses universitaires de France.

Boucheman, Albert de. 1934. 'La sedentarisation du desert de Syrie'. *L'Asie Francaise*: 140–143.

Burkhart, Johan. 1822. *Travels in Syria and the Holy Land.* London: John Murray.

Chatelard, Geraldine. 2003. 'Conflicts of Interest Over the Wadi Rum Reserve: Were They Avoidable? A Socio-Political Critique'. *Nomadic Peoples* **7**(1): 138–158.

Chatty, Dawn. 1986. *From Camel to Truck: The Bedouin in the Modern World.* New York: Vantage Press.

— 1996a. 'Employment Generation and Marginalization in Pastoral Areas in Syria and Jordan Regional Centre on Agrarian Reform and Development for the Near East' (CARDNE).

— 1996b. *Mobile Pastoralists: Development, Planning, and Social Change in Oman*. New York: Columbia University Press.

— 1998. 'Enclosures and Exclusions: Conserving Wildlife in Pastoral Areas'. *Anthropology Today* **14**(4): 2–7.

— 2010a. 'The Bedouin in Contemporary Syria: The Persistence of Tribal Authority and Control'. *Middle East Journal* **64**(1): 29–49.

— 2010b. 'Bedouin in Lebanon: The Transformation of a Way of Life or an Attitude?' *International Journal of Migration, Health and Social Care* **6**(3): 21–31.

— 2010c. *Dispossession and Displacement in the Modern Middle East.* Cambridge: Cambridge University Press.

— forthcoming. 'The Nature, Role and Impact of Bedouin Tribes in Contemporary Syria: Alternative Perceptions of Authority, Management and Control', in Uzi Rabi (ed.) *New Perspectives on Tribes, Tribalism and State Formation in the Middle East*. London: Hurst Publishers (expected 2013).

Chatty, Dawn and Marcus Colchester, eds. 2002. *Conservation and Mobile Indigenous Peoples: Displacement, Forced Settlement, and Sustainable Development*. Volume 10. Oxford and New York: Berghahn.

Chatty, Dawn, and Roland Jaubert. 2002. 'Alternative Perceptions of Authority and Control: the Desert and the Ma'moura of Syria'. *The Arab World Geographer* **5**(2): 71–73.

Cole, Donald. 1975. *Nomads of the Nomads: The Al-Murrah of the Empty Quarter*. Chicago: Aldine Publishing Company.

Cole, Donald, and Soraya Altorki. 1998. *Bedouin, Settlers and Holiday-Makers*. Cairo: American University of Cairo Press.

Debaine, Francoise and Ronald Jaubert. 2002. 'The Degradation of the Steppe, Hypotheses and Realities'. *The Arab World Geographer* **5**(2): 124–140.

Dinero, Steven. 2002. 'Image is Everything: Development of the Negev Bedouin as a Tourist Attraction'. *Nomadic Peoples* **6**(1): 69–94.

Doughty, Charles. 1888. *Travel in Arabia Deserta*. London: Jonathan Cape.

Eickelman, Dale. 1998. 'Being Bedouin: Nomads and Tribes in the Arab Social Imagination', in J. Ginat and A. Khazanov (eds.) *Changing Nomads in a Changing World*. Brighton: Sussex Academic Press.

Ellis, Jim. 1995. 'Climate variability and complex ecosystem dynamics: implications for pastoral developments', in I. Scoones (ed.) *Living with Uncertainty: New Dimensions in Pastoral Developments in Africa*. London: Intermediate Technology Publications.

Fabian, Johannes. 1983. *The Time and the Other*. New York: Columbia University Press.

Fabietti, Ugo. 2000. 'State Policies and Bedouin Adaptations in Saudi Arabia, 1900–1980', in M. Mundy and B. Musallam (eds.) *The Transformation of Nomadic Societiy in the Arab East*. Cambridge: Cambridge University Press.

Hazbun, Waleed. 2001. 'Mapping the Landscape of the "New Middle East": the Politics of Tourism Development and the Peace Process in Jordan', in G. Joffe (ed.) *Transition in Contemporary Jordan, 1989–2000*. London: Hurst.

Hobbs, Joseph. 1989. *Bedouin Life in the Egyptian Wilderness*. Austin: Texas University Press.

Khalaf, Sulayman. 1990. 'Settlement of Violence in Bedouin Society'. *Ethnology* **29**: 225–242.

Lancaster, William. 1981. *The Rwala*. Cambridge: Cambridge University Press.

Lancaster, William and Fidelity Lancaster. 1995. 'Land use and population in the area north of Karak'. *Levant* **27**:103–124.

1999. *People, Land and Water in the Arab Middle East: Environments and Landscapes in Bilad al-Sham*. Amsterdam: Harwood Academic Publishers.

Loftsdottir, Kirstin. 2002. 'Knowing What to Do in the City: WoDaaBe Nomads and Migrant Workers in Niger'. *Anthropology Today* **18**(1): 9–13.

Maktabi, Rania. 1999. 'The Lebanese Census of 1932 Revisted. Who are the Lebanese?' *British Journal of Middle Eastern Studies* **26**(2): 219–241.

Mundy, Martha and Basim Musallam, eds. 2000. *The Transformation of Nomadic Society in the Arab East*. Cambridge: Cambridge University Press.

Rae, Jonathan. 1999. 'Tribe and State: Management of the Syrian Steppe', Faculty of Anthropology and Geography, University of Oxford

Schoel, Thorsten. 2012. 'The Hsana's revenge: Syrian Tribes and Politics in thier Shaykh's Story'. *Nomadic Peoples* **15**(1): 96–113.

Spalton, Andrew, Mark Lawrence, and Stephen Brend. 1999. 'Arabian Oryx Reintroduction in Oman: Successes and Setback'. *Oryx* **32**(2): 168–175.

Triulzi, Lisa. 2001. 'Empty and Populated Landscapes: the Bedouin of the Syrian Arab Republic between "Development" and "State"'. FAO.

Introduction

Dawn Chatty and Erik Shiozaki

Plate 1. Camels going out to pasture in the Syrian desert (Al-Fed'aan)

The semi-arid land of Southwestern Asia is the heartland of Arab culture. It extends over large portions of the modern states of Saudi Arabia, Jordan, Iraq, and Syria. This region, often called Northern Arabia, is dotted with thriving and dynamic urban centres and associated agricultural peripheries such as Mecca, Amman, Damascus, Aleppo, and Baghdad. The bulk of its landmass, however, is semi-desert or steppe land, called the *Badia.* Loosely associated confederations of tribes, called the Bedouin (or *Bedu*), utilize this harsh and difficult terrain. The primary economic activity of these people was, and to an extent still is, animal husbandry by natural graze of sheep, goat and camel. This way of life, called nomadic pastoralism, has been in existence for at least three millennia. Developed over centuries of adjustment to a peculiar and harsh environment, it has been an integral and dynamic part of the general culture prevailing in Northern Arabia. This is a system consisting of three mutually dependent types of communities: urban, rural, and pastoral, each with a distinctive life mode, operating in a different setting, and contributing to the support of the other two sectors and thereby to the maintenance of the total society.

The Bedouin and their way of life have fired the imagination of historians, travellers, and poets for centuries. Much has been written about them, but all too often, the result has been highly coloured and biased. These images were derived from two sources. One was the Arab historian who viewed the Bedouin as a reminder of the greatness that once was. The second source was the European explorer and adventurer. The accounts of the European travellers in Northern Arabia generally carried vague and uninterested descriptions of the various peoples they observed. Yet rarely did they remain indifferent to the Bedouin, and the judgements they passed on them were hardly balanced. They seemed to evoke either an exaggerated distaste (Volney) or an equally coloured romanticism (Bell, Lawrence). Some described the Bedouin as quarrelsome, suspicious, and litigious. Others saw them as hospitable, brave, and independent. Among the failings of the Bedouin in the eyes of Western travellers was their idleness. The argument was that time was nowhere heavier than in the desert. Sometimes for days, the Bedouin was steeped in profound and 'corrosive' inactivity. It was then that the endless quarrels were hatched or remembered and brooded on afresh, ending in blood vendettas. Burckhart, in perhaps the most balanced account, saw both the faults and virtues of the Bedouin as complementary and conditioned by the environment and history. Their hospitality was, in his eyes, a recognition of want developed into a social grace. The stranger who came to a tent came because there was nowhere else to go. To turn a man away was equivalent to murder. Such a society could not afford to be anything but hospitable.

Arab historians, in a like manner, succumbed to similar stereotypical descriptions of the tribes of Northern Arabia. The life of the Bedouin seems to have been regarded as a shadow, a reflection of the past. The grandeur that was once their life was associated with the memory of the Umayyads, the first great Islamic dynasty. In the seventh century, some forty years after the *hijra* (the flight of Mohammed from Mecca to Medina in AD 622), the Umayyads, Meccans in origin but with strong Bedouin affiliation, took over the Islamic Caliphate. Damascus, their base, became the centre of Islam for a brilliant and dramatic century. To many Arab historians, Umayyad power represented the reaction of the Bedouin against the townsmen of Mecca and Medina. The lore of the desert, the scepticism in matters of dogma, together with imagination and good sense, were characteristics ascribed to many of the caliphs of the Umayyad dynasty. The following lines of verse, attributed to Maysoun, wife of the Umayyad Caliph, Mu'awiyya, reflected the qualities described above:

> A tent that flutters in the wind
> Is more comfortable to me than a great palace.
>
> A morsel of food in the dish from my tent
> Is tastier to me than a chunk of bread
>
> The sound of the wind coming from all sides
> Is more pleasant to me than the plucking of the tambourine
>
> The stubborn young camel following the caravan
> Is nicer to me than a swift mule.
>
> A dog barking at visitors in the night
> Is more pleasing to me than a tame cat.
>
> A simple garment of rough wool
> Is lovelier to me than a silken gown.

When Mu'awiyya, the first Umayyad Caliph, sent the heir apparent off into the *Badia*, in the charge of his Bedouin mother, to acquire a tough education in desert endurance and desert virtues, he set a fashion that subsequent caliphs followed. In one form or another, this type of schooling continued into the twentieth century, and urban families continued to send their sons to the Bedouin to make them tough and to teach them the virtues required of a noble Arab. Even today, this romantic view of the noble Bedouin remains. And one is reminded of this perception not only in written Arab histories, but also in the oral accounts of those who either experienced such an education or knew someone who did.

Both European authors as well as Arab historians have seen the Bedouin in a highly ethnocentric manner. These pastoral tribes, however, were the possessors of a heritage in their own right. The material aspects were and still are very simple, not going beyond a few implements, tools, and objects for the satisfaction of elementary needs. The non-material aspects, however, were, and to a large extent are, relatively highly developed and consist of clearly defined patterns of behaviour. These traditional ideals of conduct and behaviour, such as hospitality, generosity, community consciousness, and loyalty, originated under nomadic conditions and often are not well attuned to the circumstances of sedentary life. Although such characteristics are treated as highly admirable and praiseworthy by European and Arab urbanites, they are simply the behaviour norms that have evolved through time and have been found to be the most useful, pragmatic, and efficient in terms of the pastoral Bedouin's total environment.

At the close of World War I, Northern Arabia, nominally an Ottoman province, was partitioned by the Mandatory powers. The *Badia* was fragmented, with large chunks assigned to each of the new nations. The northern segment was awarded to the French-mandated state of Syria, the central strip was transferred to the British-mandated territories of Iraq and Jordan, while the southern wedge remained in the hands of Abdul Aziz Al-Saud. This measure, as well as the subsequent establishment of British and French administration and control in their respective regions, the development of a physical infrastructure of roads and telegraph, and finally the introduction of mechanized transport, had tremendous impact on the Bedouin tribes as well as the other two sectors of the region's ecological trilogy. To some, these developments spelled the death of the Bedouin way of life. Many of these changes, however, were quickly absorbed by the Bedouin and altered to meet the needs of their own highly adaptive system.

In spite of the Arab sentimentality towards the Bedouin, the general consensus today is that these tribes are a major obstacle to social and economic development. The recently established governments of Northern Arabia generally regard their non-sedentary populations as tribes forming a state within a state, and constituting a 'national problem'. The concern is that nationhood in the Arab world cannot be achieved on a stable and permanent basis unless the tribal segment becomes fully integrated with the rest of the nation. In this respect, concern with tribal populations is based on a desire to achieve an integrated and united nation (Awad, 1959). At the same time, pastoralism has become associated with antiprogressive forces. Administrative policies in agriculture, health, education, and land reform often appear to be obstructed by the pastoral tribes. These people are seen as a source of trouble, a backward entity that stands in the way of national progress. The only overall solution that is then suggested is the settling of the tribe, meaning the transforming of the Bedouin, who lives upon the products of the herd and flock, into a settled cultivator of the soil (Awad, I.L.O.; see also references in Philips and Barth). The key factor in this attitude, as Cunnison points out, is the 'anxiety' of many Arab administrators that pastoralism is a mode of life that is a holdover from an irrational past and therefore lacking modern rational use of the world's resources. This attitude reflects the cultural and value gap between many administrators and pastoral people within a nation-state.

The gap becomes wider when Western sources concerned with the nomad or Bedouin question are examined. Recent U.N. publications concerned with the 'nomad problem' illustrate current attitudes (*Selected Studies on Development Problems in Various Countries of the Middle East*, 1970; *Sedentarization of the Nomadic Population in the Countries of the UNESOB Region*, 1970; *Arid Lands: A Geographical Appraisal*, UNESCO, 1966; *Land Policy in the Near East,* F.A.O., 1967). These reports maintain that:

1. Pastoralism is both self-impoverishing and inimical to national development;
2. Nomadic grazing practices have led to loss of ground cover, and, as an effect of the politically drawn national borders, pastoralists take less interest in range management and conservation;
3. The habits of pastoralists isolate them from whatever educational and medical services may be available to the rest of the society.

The decision to undertake the present study evolved as even more contradictory information concerning the Bedouin came to light. Extensive library research on the 'nomad problem' revealed a particularly puzzling emphasis in the literature on 'resistance to change' of nomadic populations when compared with other societies (see Schneider, 1959; Sahlins, 1959; Weulersse, 1946; Yacoub, 1970, 1972; Coon, 1965; UNESCO, 1961, 1962, 1963; UNESOB, 1970; F.A.O., 1970; Warriner, 1959). It seemed to me the notion that people tend to resist change rather than accept change was a special bias of Western science. The question, to my mind, should have been how the Bedouin selected rather than resisted elements of change. I felt that if resistance was in fact evident, it was a symptom of a condition that threatened basic securities rather than a constant element. Consequently, I drew up a proposal for field research among a Bedouin community in Northern Arabia. I proposed to examine the role that the Bedouin community played in the general culture of the region and the extent to which pastoralism was an integral part of the whole system. Two substantive considerations dominated my field research:

1. to determine under what circumstances pastoralism is beneficial to national development; and
2. to determine whether pastoralism may or may not be the best adaptation to an arid land.

These general topics proved to be vital considerations in the course of actual field work and later in the analysis of the material forming the core of this study. I arrived in the field fully expecting to find the Bedouin community raising flocks of sheep and goat along with some herds of camel. As early as the 1930s, Mandate authorities had commented on the increasing obsolescence of the camel in Northern Arabia. Therefore, I was not particularly surprised to find that more and more Bedouin communities were abandoning camel herds altogether. Nevertheless, I had expected to find camels being used for transport, if nothing else. Instead I found that the truck had completely replaced the baggage camel. Mechanized transport had become a vital part of their existence, and gradually it became the focus of my research. Thus I found myself pursuing a new maze of questions. How had the camel, once a major tool and symbol of Bedouin life, come to be abandoned so spontaneously and with such little social dislocation? Why were trucks being so rapidly accepted? Did this new-found mobility act to further integrate them with the surrounding communities? And finally what impact did this revamped lifestyle have on former associations?

The definition of pastoralism I have used in this research is *animal husbandry by natural graze with some access to crop cultivation.* No pastoral group is entirely self-sufficient. It has interdependent and reciprocal relations to sedentary communities in adjacent areas. The pastoral adaptation to the ecological environment presupposes the presence of sedentary communities and access to their products. None of the essential utensils of metal or cured leather are produced by pastoralists. They are dependent on persons outside their own group for practically all specialized work. Furthermore,

Dawn Chatty and Erik Shiozaki

Plate 2. Young men riding camels out to pasture (Al-Fed'aan) in the Syrian desert

as a pastoral economy cannot stand alone, it must have access to some agricultural products in order to remain viable.

There are several traditional means utilized by pastoralists to guarantee that grain and other sedentary produce are accessible. A community may, if its tribal land is close enough to or within the margin of rain-fed cultivation, sow and harvest crops. More commonly, rental from oasis or agricultural land held communally by the tribe is collected in crops. At one time, tribute or *khuwa* (brotherhood tax) was exacted from sedentary farmers in return for protection from raids by their tribe or others in the surrounding areas. This tribute-raid relationship was a simple business proposition whereby the pastoralists received a needed product (grain) and the farmer acquired a scarce commodity (security). In principle, it was not very different from a more widespread relationship whereby animal products were exchanged for dates or grain. Although these activities can be regarded as secondary ones, they were at one time essential for the continued well-being of the pastoral mode of life. In turn the village and the urban community depended heavily on the pastoralists for their supplies of milk and other dairy products, mutton, and wool. Among the Bedouin, mobility has long been a distinguishing factor in tribal classification. The dignity of a Bedouin tribe was in direct proportion to its range of movement and mobility. Tribes raising camels deep in the interior of the *Badia* were the 'noble' Bedouin. The 'common' Bedouin tribes were sheep herders who had to stay near agricultural lands and necessarily found themselves at the mercy of those more wide ranging than themselves. The 'noble' camel herding Bedouin, more mobile than other pastoralists, felt they had and were widely conceded to have greater prestige than any other people in the area. However, the boundaries between these forms of pastoralism have never been rigid, but rather fluid and susceptible to modification as the environment changed.

In addition, a distinction is drawn in this study between primitive and marginal tribal societies. Primitive tribes are generally closed political units, lacking conceptual or symbolic bridges to the outside world. Marginal tribal societies, which exist at the edge of non-tribal communities, arise from the fact of their unwillingness to submit to the political authority of the urban centres, consequently withdrawing to peripheral and remote areas. The Bedouin of Northern Arabia are almost by definition marginal. Throughout the history of the region, these tribes have existed on the margin of larger political units with urban capitals and have maintained a dual relationship, partially hostile and partially symbiotic.

The political fortunes of these two units, the centralized society and the marginal Bedouin society have historically been in balanced opposition. Strength in one segment is balanced by weakness in the other. A series of drought years, for example, may force the Bedouin to the border of the settled region in search of graze for their herds. The farming community on these marginal lands, may abandon their desiccated fields to migrate to cities. Such a rural-urban migration tends to weaken centralized authority, which can no longer fill its treasury from agricultural taxes and cannot afford to maintain security on the edges of cultivation. In such cases, the marginal tribes move into the territory abandoned by cultivators, and their presence and growing political strength vis-a-vis the urban central authority is a factor promoting further abandonment of cultivation. The reverse occurs as well, when the establishment of orderly and stable central authority assumes the protection of agricultural settlements. In such cases, the tribal

Dawn Chatty and Erik Shiozaki

Plate 3. Family in front of tent in the Syrian desert (Al-Fed'aan)

sector is pushed back deeper into the semi-arid desert region. During the eighteenth and nineteenth centuries, for example, a tremendous push north westward by the Aneza and Shammar Bedouin tribes is recorded. As Ottoman central authority in the area weakened, the Aneza and Shammar encroached further into cultivated areas, disturbing traditional ecological niches in the countryside. The expansion of these Bedouin tribes was checked only in the last one hundred years. This occurred in direct response to the establishment of stable central government. Throughout the last period of Ottoman rule (1850–1918), the Inter War Mandate (1919–1943), and independent national rule (post-1943), government control and authority has been gradually extended over most areas of Northern Arabia.

This study is organized in two sections. Part 1 seeks to provide the general ecological, political, and economic foundation for an analysis of the Bedouin and their role in the modern states of Jordan, Syria, Iraq, and Saudi Arabia which encompass the geographic region of Northern Arabia. In chapter 1, a superficial gleaning of a complicated history is attempted only insofar as it sheds light on the Bedouin as important political actors in the Arabian Peninsula. The cyclical nature of pastoralism and the associated ecological factors form a background to the major historical process, the westward expansion of Bedouin tribes to the fringes of the marginal cultivated land, during the eighteenth and nineteenth centuries. This expansion displaced numerous minor tribes as well as settled agricultural populations, resulting in major shifts in populations, relations of competition and conflict, and finally the utilization of new ecological niches. Chapter 2 deals with more recent political and economic factors in the Bedouin universe at the close of World War I. After the creation of the French and British Mandate over Northern Arabia, general security was restored and Bedouin political and military power was severely restricted. Some Bedouin tribes began a retreat deeper into the *Badia* to escape the arm of authority. Other Bedouin groups, accepting the separate status accorded them by the mandatory authority, remained near the margins of cultivation and adapted their life mode to better suit the new human and physical environment of Northern Arabia.

Part 2 is derived primarily from field notes and deals with the Bedouin from a closer perspective as individuals and as small tribal communities. The transformation of the, at one time, paramount political and military strength of the Bedouin into economic power and, to a degree, moral authority is examined. Chapter 3 deals with the complex of behaviour patterns that characterize Arab society in general, and Bedouin society in particular. These traits form the backdrop for an analysis of tribal organization and leadership and the extent to which the Bedouin and their leaders have selectively adapted to the political, social, and technological developments of the region as a whole. Chapter 4 provides a description and analysis of lower levels of organization in Bedouin society, namely the family and lineage. The initial impact of the truck and the subsequent changes that were generated are examined. Particular emphasis is placed on the permutations within the household, the simultaneous growth of individualism at the expense of lineage organization, and finally the continuities and discontinuities of sheep raising pastoralism. Chapter 5 investigates the growing spheres of economic activity resulting from the Bedouin's new-found mobility and the ways in which these pursuits have become essential elements of the regional economy of Northern Arabia. Once the novelty of motorized transport had been absorbed, new economic horizons in the related fields of commerce and transport were followed. Without fundamentally restructuring their society, the Bedouin modernized even more, thus underscoring the unique nature of the pastoral adaptation.

Introduction

Over the past fifteen years, among the Bedouin tribes in Syria, Jordan, Iraq, and Saudi Arabia, the Datsun and Toyota half-ton trucks have become a common sight parked beside a tent encampment, more common in fact, than baggage camels. These vehicles now serve to transport households and livestock from one camp to another, and to carry water to the herds when they are deep in the *Badia.* In addition, the truck has greatly facilitated the commercialization of sheep raising. It is used to carry feed supplement to the herds, to convey the fattened sheep to market without weight loss. And finally it provides for easy and continuous relations between the village and tribal encampment, permitting many Bedouin families to undertake secondary work activities such as wage labour in settlements near their tribal grazing lands. The Bedouin today are effecting their own widespread integration into the regional economy without a major restructuring of their society. It was not necessary, as many had believed, for the pastoralists to settle and become cultivators in order to modernize and become integrated into the regional economy. The process of adaptation whereby this integration was made possible reveals the fundamental importance of livestock for these pastoral populations. It is livestock that holds a dominant place in their system of values. To the cultivator, the soil yields food, and food is essential for life, but, to the pastoralist, it is the herd that yields food, and not the soil.

The universe of the individual Bedouin is no longer the *Badia,* but the whole of the Middle East. As a population, however, their future depends upon the question of political integration into the nation-state. The governments of Syria, Jordan, Saudia Arabia, and Iraq have yet to recognize the widespread integration of the Bedouin into the regional economy. And perhaps recalling the anarchic activities of the Bedouin prior to independence, these governments are still trying to settle them and turn them into controllable cultivators. The Bedouin, in turn, refuse to give up their way of life. So long as they can make a profit from the herd, they will continue to do so. It is ironic that many of the cultural values at the foundation of Bedouin life are upheld as ideals of behaviour in Arab society, while the Bedouin's attachment to pastoralism as a way of life is viewed through unsympathetic if not contemptuous eyes.

~ 1 ~

The Bedouin and How They Came to Be Where They Are

The word 'Bedouin' had for centuries – and has, even today – two meanings. The first of these is the 'noble' tribes whose daring accomplishments are associated with the rise and spread of the Islamic empire. The second meaning, however, is the nomads, whom the Arabs consider generally to be nothing more than gypsies (*Nawwar*) that roam throughout the region selling their wares and services to whoever will buy. This ambiguous concept of the Bedouin derives from an incomplete grasp of the nature of the pastoral adaptation to the geographical and ecological realities of Northern Arabia. It is essential, therefore, to gain some understanding of the importance of terrain, water, pasture, and human settlement in pastoral nomadic society. These are the fundamental constraints at work in shaping Bedouin life.

Northern Arabia contains two major geographic units. The first is the Mediterranean coastline, a narrow strip of fertile land stretching roughly from Aleppo to the Gulf of Aqaba. The second is the arid Arabian Plateau, a tilted block of ancient rock extending in an arc from the Red Sea to the Persian Gulf. (See map 2)

Only two portions of the Arabian Plateau are pure desert (*Sahra*), where there is so little vegetation that neither humans nor animals can live. To the south there is the *Rub'al-Khali,* and to the north, there is the *Nefud*, both linked by a narrow belt of dunes about fifteen miles wide. Most of the plateau is not desert, but arid (*Badia*) in the sense that water is the most decisive limiting factor in supporting life. Where water is scarce, plant, animal and human life are sparsely scattered. Where water is abundant, all three are heavily concentrated.

Several categories of terrain based on the availability of water are found in this arid region:

1. Where water is available underground and can be tapped for the irrigation of small patches of land and gardens. This type of terrain is called an oasis and may consist of a single settlement or be large enough to include a community of settlements.

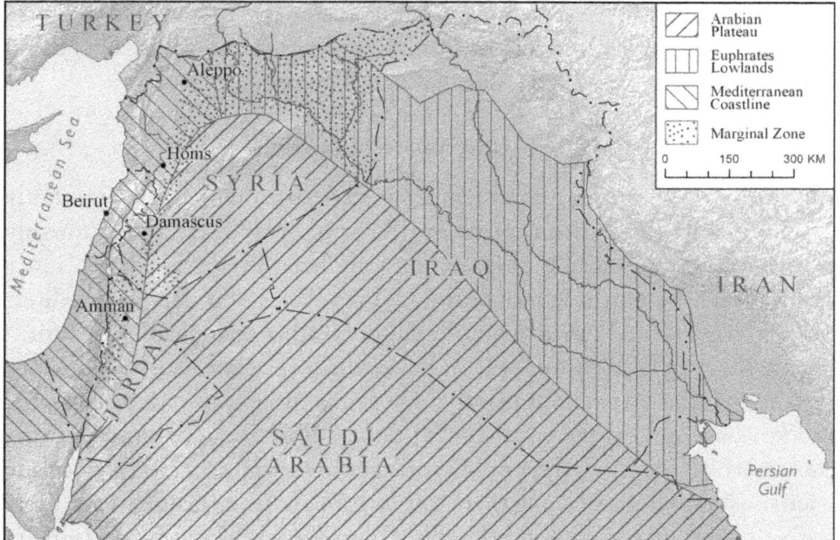

Map 2. Geographical units and marginal zone

2. Where rain in a given spot is predictable enough to warrant dry farming of crops, but not sufficiently reliable to support permanent human settlement. This type of terrain lies primarily along the border zone between cultivated and pastoral lands.

3. Where there is enough scattered rain water to produce sporadic vegetation for grazing, but where settled agriculture in any one spot is impossible. Thus between the isolated and widely scattered agricultural oases and dry farming regions on the fringes of the *Badia* there is terrain good only for herding grazing animals from one transitory pasture to another.

Nomadic pastoralism has prevailed mainly in the north and centre of the Arabian Plateau. At its core, migration was, and still is, determined by a combination of seasonal and areal variability in the location of pasture and water. Because water and grass could be in short supply in a particular area at the same time that it was abundant elsewhere, survival of both herd and herders made movement from deficit to surplus areas both logical and necessary. Thus each group sought to control a territory that contained sufficient resources to sustain communal life. The relatively stable dominance, over a period of time, of such territory by a group of genealogically related agnatic segments identified a pastoral nomadic tribe.

The Mediterranean Coastline

Along the northern part of the Arabian Plateau runs the predominantly agricultural Mediterranean coastline. This strip of land, extending roughly from the ancient Antioch to Gaza, has long been the centre of sedentary civilization. The northern part of the Arabian Plateau borders the Mediterranean coastline and can ecologically support either agriculture in the form of extensive dry farming or nomadic pastoralism of camel, sheep and goat. It is this zone that throughout history has been contested, and its agricultural borders have undergone considerable fluctuation. The relationship of the pastoral tribes with the larger urban and agrarian settlements has historically been most pronounced along this frontier. As no pastoral group was entirely self-sufficient, it was tied in relations of interdependence and reciprocity to sedentary communities in adjacent areas. Sometimes this was expressed as a trade relation with scattered oases in the *Badia* itself, where animal products were exchanged for grain and dates. Just as often, it was expressed in a tribute/raid relationship with the sedentary farmers along the fringes of the frontier areas. Here tribute (*khuwa*) was exacted from the farmers, generally in the form of crops, in return for protection from raids (*ghazu*). This relationship was a simple proposition whereby the pastoralists received a needed product (grain) and the farmer gained a scarce service (security). Thus, throughout the history of the region, pastoral tribes have existed on the margins of larger political units with urban centres and agricultural hinterlands, maintaining a dual relationship partially hostile and partially symbiotic.

The political fortunes of these two units, the centralized society and the marginal pastoral population, as a rule, have been in balanced opposition. Strength in one segment has always been balanced by weakness in the other. When urban central authority was strong, it could protect its agricultural hinterland and prevent the pastoral tribes from encroaching on the agricultural communities and exacting tribute from them. A series of drought years, on the other hand, would force the pastoral tribes to the edges of the frontier zone in desperate search for pasture. At the same time, farmers would abandon their desiccating fields and move to the urban centres. This rural-urban exodus would further weaken the central authority, who would be unable to collect agricultural taxes and thereby maintain security on the edges of cultivation. In such cases, the marginal pastoral tribes moved into the territory abandoned by the cultivators and their presence and growing strength vis-a-vis the urban centres became a factor for further abandonment of cultivation. This was the basis of what is often called the cyclical nature of pastoralism: fluctuating expansion and contraction of pastoralism along the frontiers of cultivated land.

Such a pattern of life, however, presupposed the domestication of the camel, which alone was uniquely capable of forming the basis for large-scale pastoral nomadic existence in the arid steppe lands of Northern Arabia. The camel's domestication appears to have been relatively late. Available evidence, from bones, wall drawings, inscriptions, and written accounts do not definitively reveal where, when, or why camels became domesticated (Miksell). Mesopotamian records establish the camel as a domestic animal during the Assyrian era (1,000–500 BC), and they figure in the bronze gates of Balwat in the reign of Shalmaneser III (858–824 BC). By 600 BC camel raising was a well-established tradition in Northern Arabia.

Once the camel had been domesticated, it carried with it the potentialities of a major social revolution. Camels allowed their herders greater mobility than any other pastoral animals being able to tolerate extremes of heat and lack of water, to thrive on desert plants beyond the capacity of other domestic animals and to cover greater distances between watering places. The only other animal as tough, fast, and well suited to the arid steppe was the ass. The camel, however, was also a great beast of burden, unrivalled by any other domesticated animal in Northern Arabia. These features of endurance and strength gave the camel raising pastoralists a potential predominance over the sheep raising populations as well as the oases and marginal zone cultivators. This potential predominance rapidly came to be expressed in a system of social stratification. The highly mobile camel herding tribes who moved outside the range of settled power considered themselves to be the 'noble' Bedouin. The sheep raising tribes, who had to remain near the margins of settled cultivation with their herds and often found themselves dominated by the camel raising tribes, were considered to be the 'common' Bedouin.

The arid steppe land of Northern Arabia lay between the three vast agricultural regions of Iraq, Syria and Yemen. Syria and Iraq formed the main portion of the Fertile Crescent, while Yemen was the site of numerous agricultural kingdoms. During the fifth century BC, Yemen was a great commercial capital. The pastoral nomadic Bedouin were, at that time, clients of the Yemenite kings for whom they carried out overland trade, bringing incense and other southern products to the Fertile Crescent.

Originally this overland trade route ran just inland on the interior side of the coastal mountain range of Western Arabia. The camel raising Bedouin of Northern Arabia supplied the means of transport, but there is no evidence that they controlled the trade or reaped its profits. Between the third and fifth centuries AD, however, a complex series of technological breakthroughs gave the Bedouin the means of converting their potential control of the caravan trade into real control. These included the Northern Arabian riding saddle as well as the metal sword and spear. As the Bedouin gained in military and thus economic strength, they took up new routes, which crossed the Arabian Plateau in the middle and around its northern fringe. The termini of the incense route shifted from the Fertile Crescent to the Bedouin's own oasis settlements. These were then built up into prosperous caravan cities such as Petra, Tudmor (Palymyra), and Mecca. As a consequence, greater wealth flowed into the hands of the Bedouin, leading to more intimate commercial ventures in the settled lands. These ventures then led to a revolution in the transport economy of the entire region (Bulliet). The use of wheeled vehicles such as the ox-drawn wagon was entirely abandoned, and their place was taken by the pack camel and the ass. Since the camel was exclusively a product of the pastoral economy, the Bedouin rapidly became integral elements in settled society.

By the end of the fifth century AD, the Bedouin were looked upon for military support by each of the super powers on the margins of the Arabian Plateau. To the east, the Persian (Zoroastrian, Sasanian), to the north the Byzantine (Christian, Roman), and in the extreme south the Himyar (Yemenite) empires struggled with each other to assert their dominance over the Arabian Peninsula. The Himyar supported a great Bedouin confederation in Central Arabia under the leadership of the Kinda tribe. The Byzantines subsidized the Ghassanid on the southern borders of Syria. While at Hira near the Euphrates, the Persians financed the Lakhmids, who controlled the end of the Arabian caravan route to the Fertile Crescent.

Under the stimulus of the international competition of the great powers, money poured into Bedouin hands, and their caravan cities flourished. The most important caravan centre of Western and Central Arabia, at the junction of the major trade routes, was Mecca in the Hijaz. In the early sixth century ad, a tribe of Bedouin was brought together called the 'Qurayish'. Under the leadership of Qusayy, they took over the springs at Mecca and established their control over the centre. They monopolized the north south trade, fostered pilgrimages, and rapidly institutionalized the pre-eminence of Mecca over all other centres in religious forms. Mohammed was born in this community, of the Hashim section of the Qurayish tribe. He thus belonged to a settled Arab community of Bedouin origin, and his first religious message was for them. At first he preached only to a small circle of friends and relatives. But step by step he acquired the authority of a military leader. He began to exhibit his qualities of political genius as he adapted all the powerful Bedouin traditions of personal honour, brotherhood, and tribal solidarity to strengthen his community. When Mohammed first began to recite his message, the Bedouin were despised and feared by their settled neighbours. Yet before Mohammed's death twenty years later, these bands of tribesmen had been welded into a single dynamic nation.

The expansion of the infant Islamic Caliphate began with a series of probing raids into Mesopotamia. At first the fighting was done only by the Bedouin warriors. At this stage, the Bedouin along with their settled kin formed the ruling class among Moslems, and the Islamic state was essentially a Bedouin confederation. The idea that non-Bedouin should become Moslems, although clearly sanctioned by the *Koran*, was still so unfamiliar that any convert who was not a full member by descent of a Bedouin tribe had to become a client of one of them (*Mawal*). Persians, Egyptians, Berbers, and even Arabs – by language – who failed to prove their full membership in the Bedouin tribal group became *Mawali* tribes. By AD 700, the vast expanse of the Islamic conquest demanded a change in policy. Bedouin manpower was no longer sufficient, and the *Mawali* tribes were recruited to fight. The conquest of the great Persian and Byzantine empires was achieved with amazing speed. As the Bedouin and the *Mawali* tribes conquered and intermarried with non-Bedouin, some gradually gave up their pastoral way of life and adopted a sedentary existence.

Over the course of the next few centuries, the Islamic state came to encompass increasing numbers of non-Bedouin and non-Arab populations. Those who had left the arid steppe lands of Northern Arabia soon forgot that way of life, and totally adopted sedentary values. Supreme among these was a general disdain for the pastoral mode of existence. The upper classes, however, in an effort to justify their place in society, attempted to maintain some link with the original conquering Bedouin tribes. The fourteenth-century Arab sociologist who analyzed this phenomenon wrote: 'Those Arabs who took up a more sedentary life, however, found themselves, in their quest for more fertile lands and rich pastures, crowding in on other people—all of which led to a mixture of blood and confusion of genealogies ... Hence tribal names tended to be cast aside ... and with them all traces of tribal solidarity. The Bedouin, however, continued as they had always been.' (Ibn Khaldun 1958:100) Thus, members of the urban ruling classes had great pride in their Bedouin origin, however diluted or questionable their genealogy might be. Nevertheless, they were inclined to refer disparagingly to those who retained their pastoral way of life and refused to settle down. The Bedouin – and their role in the expansion of the Islamic empire – was idealized, while the actual population, which carried on its age-old system of nomadic pastoralism in the steppe lands of Northern Arabia, came to be regarded in an ambivalent if not critical manner by the rest of the Islamic world.

In Northern Arabia, the frontiers of pastoralism continued to oscillate in response to the waxing and waning of central authority in the settled regions. When disintegration of urban Arab rule set in during the eleventh century, a Turkish nomadic people, the Seljuks, moved into the region from the east. Shortly thereafter, the Frankish Crusaders descended on the area from the north, defeating the Seljuks and establishing four feudal Latin states along the Mediterranean coastlines in Edessa, Antioch, Tripoli and Jerusalem. Eventually, a Kurdish force under the leadership of Salah-id-Din was formed to oppose the Crusaders. After the Battle of Acre, in 1192, a peace settlement was concluded, leaving only a small coastal strip under the control of the Crusaders.

In 1240, a Mongol invasion from the east occurred, led by Hulaga Khan, who sacked Baghdad, Aleppo, and Damascus. This force was finally repulsed by Baybar, one of the leading *Mamluks* (captured Turks, Kurds, Mongols, exiles and refugees who had become incorporated into the Moslem military and ruling class). One century later in 1387, another Mongol invasion occurred directed by Timur (Tamerlane) who captured Aleppo, Hama, Homs, Baalbek, and Damascus. With the devastation of Timur, anarchy prevailed in the region accompanied by droughts, plagues, and famines. The agricultural countryside was deserted. A major invasion or expansion of Bedouin tribes then took place from the *Badia* of Northern Arabia into the lower Euphrates and Mediterranean coastline, resulting in mass rural migrations to the major urban centres.

During the sixteenth century, after the reconquest of the region by the Othmani Turks (Sultan Selim I,1517), Northern Arabia again experienced a period of prosperity and an expansion of agriculture into the border zone between the Mediterranean coastline and the Arabian Plateau. With this agricultural expansion, a number of Bedouin tribes were pushed back deeper into the Northern Arabian Plateau leaving only Al-Fadl, Mawali, and the Haddiddiin sheep raising tribes in the northern segment of the *Badia.* At this stage the distinction between 'noble' and 'common' Bedouin tribes began to break down. The Mawali and Al-Fadl both claimed to be of 'noble' tribes (see Oppenheim, 1939). However these were sheep raising tribes and technically 'common' tribes. Yet they were subservient to no one. They had mastery of the *Badia.* They were the ones who exacted tribute (*khuwa*) or threatened raids (*ghazu*). They were, in practice, patron and thus 'noble' tribes.

The middle of the seventeenth century saw Ottoman military presence in the desert border areas being withdrawn, particularly in the area between Damascus and Homs in order to support Mohammed IV's (1648–1687) war against Austria (Hourani, 1946). The Ottoman defeat outside of Vienna in 1683 was a turning point for the Arab provinces. With much of its military presence drawn out of the Middle East, its authority in outlying provinces grew weaker, especially on the fringes of the *Badia.* Once again villages were abandoned and fertile plains were turned to wasteland. During this period, plagues and famine again occurred, killing as many as two million people (Nutting, 1964).

Volney, a traveller in the region during the 1780s, remarked that, as a result of misgovernment, great parts of the provinces were wasted, and, although 3,200 villages were registered in government records, fewer than 400 could be found by the tax collector. 'The traveller meets with nothing but houses in ruin, cisterns rendered useless, and fields abandoned. Those who cultivate them are fled.' (Volney, 1787: 377–379).

With the power and effectiveness of the Ottoman Empire greatly reduced, numerous camel raising Bedouin tribes from the interior of the *Badia* began to drift northward. This expansion was to continue for nearly

150 years, pushing the frontiers of pastoralism west through the borders of the Mediterranean coastline. The tribal expansion was in two distinct phases, of which the second phase resulted in the conquest of the northern *Badia* frontier and the Euphrates region by the great Aneza and Shammar camel raising Bedouin tribes. The initial impetus behind the first phase of the Bedouin expansion was not fully understood. Perhaps the interior of the *Badia* was experiencing drought or overpopulation (Burckhart, 1831; Weulersse, 1946). Arab historians make particular mention of this expansion of Bedouin tribes in the direction of the Euphrates because it seriously menaced the pilgrims going to or returning from Mecca. According to these historical interpretations, the former strength of the sheep raising Mawali Bedouin tribe had been shrinking since the end of the seventeenth century. As a result, a power vacuum existed in the northern *Badia* attracting other Bedouin tribes to move in and take over. Most certainly the relative emptiness of the *Badia* at this time and the almost absolute lack of government authority in the region must have been a strong inducement for the tribes to migrate north.

The second phase of the Bedouin invasion was a direct reaction against the growing strength of an important Unitarian or Wahhabi reform movement in Central Arabia. Some Bedouin tribes refused to submit to the exigencies of the political system that had been formed by the Al-Saud under the banner of the Wahhabi. At the end of the seventeenth century, the 'noble' camel raising Shammar confederacy based near Hail and the Jebel Shammar moved north across the *Badia* and attacked the region of Damascus. Unable to penetrate, they turned and crossed the *Badia* in the direction of Tudmor (Palmyra) and finally moved on to the Mawali-controlled Homs-Hama region. Their efforts to take over were strongly resisted by the Mawali. The Shammar then turned east and settled on the grazing land in the Euphrates region (Oppenheim, 1939).

The genealogies of these two tribes illustrated the characteristic way in which Bedouin society tended to reduce all relations to an idiom of kinship. The Mawali Bedouin have for centuries been associated with the sheep raising Al-Fadl tribe and the camel raising Shammar Bedouin. There are varying written interpretations concerning the origin of these three tribes (Oppenheim, 1939; Glubb, 1942; Muller, 1931). One popular account has it that the Fadl were for centuries masters of the region between Homs and Hama. At the time of the rise of Ottoman control over Northern Arabia, the Emir of Al-Fadl and a number of tribal lineages attempted to escape the reaches of government authority by moving into the Bekaa Valley and the Golan. The remaining lineages of the tribe stayed in the Homs region and took the name 'Mawali'. The Shammar, according to one curious interpretation, were originally of Mawali origin. The claim is that, once after an incident in the *Badia*, several Mawali left their tribe and took refuge with the Shammar near Jebel Shammar. As they were of 'noble' origin, they soon took over the Shammar leadership and shortly thereafter moved north to carry out vengeance against their Mawali relations in the north (Oppenheim, 1939).

These interpretations of genealogy were meant to explain the past. In fact, they acted to rationalize or, more often, to justify present conditions of inter-tribal strength and weakness. In all these geneaological histories 'noble' was a term used by the Bedouin to describe tribes that could trace their apical ancestor back to Qais and Yemen (or Adnan and Qahtan, the older term), the brothers believed to have founded the Arab 'nation'. The implicit assumption, of course, was that 'noble' tribes raised camels and 'common' tribes, whose origins were unknown, raised sheep.

At the beginning of the eighteenth century, the first tribes of the 'noble' camel raising Aneza confederation appeared on the margins of the *Badia* and laid siege to the region around Damascus. Finding this assault ineffective, they turned to the Nebek region. The Hassanna tribe of the Aneza then stopped and took over pasture land in the region of Homs. The Fed'aan, another Aneza tribe, continued north to the grazing areas around Hama. These two tribes then allied themselves with the Mawali tribe and proceeded to push the rival Shammar tribes farther across the Euphrates into the *Jezireh* (arid steppe land east of the Euphrates River).

Throughout this period of expansion into the margins of cultivated land, some branches of the Aneza and Shammar tribes remained in the interior of the *Badia* and continued to follow their traditional way of life. Camels continued to be raised as a major economic pursuit for subsistence and for caravan transit. These camel raising Bedouin were the masters of the *Badia* itself. They provided the means of transport, the men handling the animals, and the guides who had the vital knowledge of routes, water places, and existing pastures for the animals. The Bedouin thus held a position based on all the privileges of monopoly. They levied heavy charges and extracted regular fees from every caravan crossing the *Badia*. No purpose, however holy, exempted the traveller from the reality of either buying protection or being raided. Even the annual pilgrim caravan to the holy cities of Mecca and Medina was not exempted.

During the eighteenth century, the governor of Damascus was considered the pilgrimage commander by the Ottoman authority in Istanbul. A sum of money called the *maal-al-badal* was assigned to the governor each year in order to pay for troops to escort the annual pilgrimage caravan to Mecca. Some Bedouin tribes along this route also received payment, mainly to procure safe passage through their regions. Other tribes, like the Aneza tribes, received additional sums for transporting the pilgrims and their baggage to the Hijaz.

There were times, however, when the commander of the pilgrimage tried to withhold part of the sum allotted for safe passage. In such cases, the Bedouin retaliated by attacking the caravan, generally on the return trip (Rafiq, 1966). At that moment, the caravan would be heavily loaded with merchandise. It would also be the last opportunity for the Bedouin to obtain their full payment from the pilgrimage commander.

The governor of Damascus generally made payments to the larger, more powerful Aneza tribes not only for facilitating the passage of the Pilgrimage caravan, but also for safeguarding the normal trade caravans that crossed the *Badia* between Damascus and Baghdad. The smaller, less threatening tribes either paid tribute to the governor or were periodically disciplined by his soldiers. One example was the Ottoman punitive expedition in 1755 against Al-Fadl in the Golan. These smaller Bedouin tribes were often defeated and their sheep then sold on the Damascus market at very high prices. In spite of these punitive and conciliatory measures, the Ottoman authorities were unable to check the generally anarchic raiding of the Bedouin, nor were they able to gain completely secure passage across the *Badia.*

By the early nineteenth century, the Aneza tribes had established themselves firmly in the *Badia.* Whatever the cause of the expansion, their movements into the Eastern Plains and border zones were marked by inter-tribal strife, feud, and war, which affected the entire region. Once the Aneza had successfully pushed the Shammar across the Euphrates, they began to fight amongst themselves to divide the newly conquered pasture lands. The Hassanna near Homs and the Fed'aan near Aleppo were followed by other Aneza tribes. These included the Sbaa', the Wuld Ali, some Amarat, and lastly the Ruwalla (see figure 1).

These inter-tribal wars, particularly during the 1860–1870s, greatly disturbed the security of the region. Institutions such as *khuwa* (tribute) and *ghazu* (raid) changed in nature. Ghazu lost its traditional characteristic of sport or game and assumed an almost desperate nature among the tribes and settlements in the region. Several large cities like Aleppo and Hama were raided and pillaged. Khuwa, which was being collected in greater quantities, no longer presented a 'guarantee of security' as it had in the interior of the *Badia* (Bell, 1907). It became simply extortion.

The uncontested mastery of the Aneza over the *Badia* can be traced back to the 1830s, when Ali Pasha was governor of Baghdad. During that period, he enlisted the help of the Aneza to control the Shammar Bedouin. With his support, the Aneza attacked the area of the Shammar near Baghdad. They proceeded to completely conquer and ravage that territory as well as to paralyze all commerce and transport in the region.

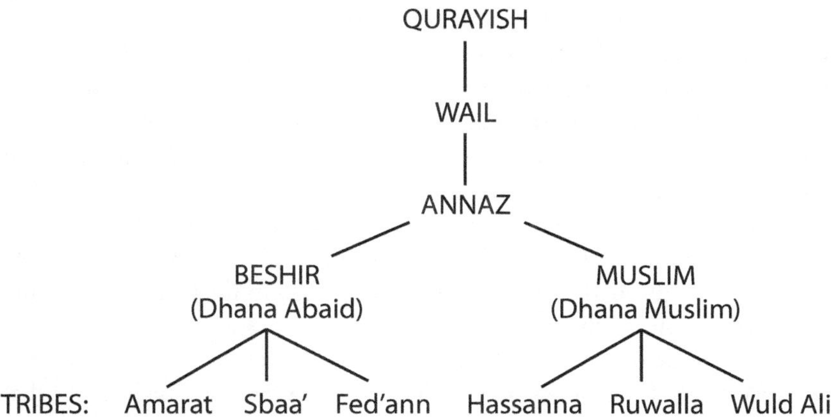

Figure 1. Aneza confederation of tribes

See *Handbook of Nomads, Semi-Nomadic, Semi-Sedentary, and Sedentary Tribes of Syria*, G.S.I., Headquarters, 9th Army, 1942.

By the 1860s, the tribal struggle over pasture rights, water rights, and influence on the border zone from Aleppo to the Hauran began to constitute a serious disruptive element in the Ottoman government's hold over the region. A period of reform was then initiated under Abdul Hamid II, and new methods were attempted in order to restore Ottoman military authority. Thus a period of greater safety and economic benefit for cultivators began to take shape.

Small forts and police stations were established along the borders of marginal cultivated lands as far as Deir-ez-Zor. The Ottoman then introduced a policy that encouraged the smaller tribes to risk raiding the large Aneza tribes. Tribal feuds were provoked by Ottoman agents, and Turkish troops with modern arms were lent to one side or another. The most striking example of this policy was the last major battle among the tribes of the Aneza confederacy. In 1875, Sattam Sha'laan of Al-Ruwalla hired Turkish troops to fight the Sbaa', who were thereby overwhelmingly defeated. It was a case of rifles against lances.

Agricultural expansion by indigenous peasants, landowners, and immigrants was actively sponsored by the Ottoman. Turkish soldiers armed with Winchester rifles and breechloading Sniders manned new border garrisons, giving the agriculturalists the security they needed to increase in numbers and strength. The most aggressive of these new settlers were the Circassians fleeing the Russian occupation of the Caucasus. After 1870, Circassian villages sprang up near the *Badia* border zone from its northern frontier as far south as Amman. They occupied and cultivated the land, while acting as a successful buffer against the Bedouin. The Druze, always effective in protecting their villages, pushed the frontiers of settlement farther back. Efforts to break their power in south central Lebanon resulted in a migration of the Druze to the Jebel Druze and Suweida around 1860. There they established and maintained themselves in the face of opposition from the Bedouin tribes.

In the area of Hama and Salamiyeh, new settlements pushing out into the very edge of the *Badia* were formed by Alawite, Circassian, and other peasant communities. In the districts of the Hauran, Homs, Hama, and Aleppo, peasants began to return and reclaim their former villages. And sheep raising Bedouin tribes in these areas such as the Fadl, the Mawali, and the Haddiddiin were evicted, or surrounded by agricultural communities. On a visit to the Orontes Valley north of the Lebanon, Gertrude Bell reported that, although it was still frequented in dry seasons by 'a few sheikhs of the Hassanna and Al-Ruwalla', the bulk of the Bedouin were being driven out by cultivation (Bell, 1907). Some tribal sections, particularly in the area of Aleppo, began to settle and take up agriculture. Examples included several hundred tents of the Wuld Ali, some Haddiddiin, and some Mawali sections. Other tribal sections began to combine pastoralism with agriculture.

In 1865, the Ottoman government awarded Jed'aan ibn Muheid of the Fed'aan tribe the income of twenty villages in the Aleppo district. As few members of his tribe would settle and become farmers, he hired peasants to work the land for him as sharecroppers. Originally intended as an inducement for tribal settlement, the Ottoman land title simply turned this tribal sheikh into a privately wealthy landowner as well. A similar situation occurred in the Golan, where Al-Fadl were granted permission to register long-contested land in their names. Al-Fadl tribal leaders then set about converting this new prestige as 'landowners' into power and influence over the peasants in the region, many of whose villages they were later able to buy.

The Ottoman government also began to assist settlers by granting special privileges and tax remissions. Vast areas that had recently been secured by Ottoman military rule near the frontier were declared state domain, and settlers on these lands were granted special terms. Thus the most recent Bedouin pastoral expansion or invasion into the frontier agricultural areas of the *Badia* began to be pushed back east by the 'Agricultural Eastward Movement' of the late nineteenth and early twentieth century (see map 2).

The cyclical nature of pastoral expansion and retreat in the face of strong or weak central government is clearly illustrated by the three historical examples given. Nevertheless, Ibn Khaldun's interpretation of this process differs somewhat. In his *Muqaddimah*, he suggests that the situation is more a case of Bedouin who conquer, take over, and then succumb to the 'luxuries and enfeebling evils' of urban civilization. These then are taken over by a new wave of unspoiled Bedouin riding out from the desert. Perhaps. Yet what appears most striking thus far is the long tradition among the Bedouin of urban ties and relations. Throughout history, from the Umayyad period to the present, Bedouin leaders have maintained close relations with centres of power without succumbing irreversibly to that way of life. Even at the beginning of the twentieth century this association was evident. In 1907, Gertrude Bell wrote, 'In Damascus, the sheikhs of the richer tribes have their town houses; you may meet Muhammed of the Hassanneh or Bassem of the Beni Rashid peacocking down the bazaars in embroidered cloaks and purple and silver kerchiefs ... striding through the crowds that part to give them passage, as if Damascus were their town. And so it is, for it was the first capital of the Bedouin Arab Caliphs outside the Hijaz and it holds and remembers the greatest Arab tradition.' (Bell, 1907: 134–135).

Throughout the last period of Ottoman rule (1850–1918), new political ideas were emerging, and the concept of Arab nationalism was gaining support. The sheikhly Bedouin elite, with their long tradition of contact with important urban figures, became involved in the struggle. The leaders of three Bedouin tribes in close proximity to Damascus, the Ruwalla, and Fadl, and the Hassanna, were particularly active. Their involvement with the various Ottoman, English, and French agents marked a shift in emphasis from their earlier conduct, which was primarily to assert their independence from central authority, and their hegemony over a particular region or tribe.

From the turn of the century until the establishment of the Inter War Mandate (1919–1943), these leaders were intimately involved in the international power struggle taking place over Northern Arabia. The Fadl threw their support behind King Faysal's movement for independence from Ottoman rule. Nuri Sha'laan of the Ruwalla had, in the early 1910s, cooperated with the Ottoman authorities and was reported to have received a monthly allowance of 20,000 gold pounds from General Ahmad Jamal Pasha. In 1910, after a clash with an Ottoman official, he was exiled to Spain. He returned to Damascus in 1916 in time to accept Lawrence's English overtures and join in the support of King Faysal. The sheikh of the Hassanna had been a participant in the general Arab revolt against the Ottoman as well. After his death, his son Trad then took an active part in the movement, and, in September 1918, both Sheikh Trad and Nuri Sha'laan entered Damascus with the troops of King Faysal.

After the defeat of King Faysal and the establishment of a British and French mandate over the former Ottoman province, each of these sheikhly families and their supporters went their separate ways. The Hassanna continued their interest in seeing the establishment of an independent nation. Sheikh Trad, interviewed by members of the King-Crane Commission, is reported to have demanded the return of the land. 'We do not want to see English or French soldiers in our country.' Al-Fadl leaders, protesting against the establishment of a French mandate over their territory, went into exile in the newly created British mandate state of Jordan. The Sha'laan of Al-Ruwalla vacillated between both the French and the English until finally they reached an agreement with the French Délégué, Colonel Catroux, to safeguard caravans in the *Badia* and to secure peace among the tribes against a monthly stipend of two thousand gold pounds.

Thus, during the two decades prior to the French and British mandates over Northern Arabia, the Bedouin sheikhs involved themselves in affairs other than simply intertribal struggles. They became involved in issues of wider political implication. Their base of support was the *Badia*, and, as long as they remained involved with the issues pertaining directly to it, they had appreciable influence. Once they entered an arena far removed from the *Badia*, they were at a loss. The foundation of their support and interest shifted then from a political base to an economic one.

Aside from the issue of political involvement, the Bedouin were now facing a crisis of major significance. As government control spread further into areas they had controlled for a century or more, the tribes had the choice of either retreating into the *Badia* or accommodating themselves to the agricultural encroachment. Sheep, the traditional herding animal of the 'common' tribes, began gradually to replace camels as the major herding animals of 'noble' tribes such as the Hassanna, the Fed'aan, and the Ruwalla. The pattern, motivated by underlying economic and ecological considerations, came to be widespread throughout the region, particularly in present-day Saudi Arabia, Iraq, Syria, and Jordan. The longstanding differentiation between 'noble' tribes as camel raisers and 'common' tribes as sheep raisers began to blur. This adaptation was viewed by many as a sign of decadence in Bedouin life, and a step in the direction of permanent settlement. In fact, it demonstrated the vitality of the pastoral mode of existence in the new balance that was being created between animal husbandry and cultivation. This change in herding animals, which began in the 1920s and 1930s, was just as dramatic an adaptation as the shift from camel to truck transport a half-century later.

~ 2 ~

Pacification of the Bedouin in Northern Arabia

By 1914, Northern Arabia had been a part of the Ottoman Empire for four hundred years. During most of this long period, the region was governed as little more than a remote province of a foreign power. The territory witnessed almost no material development, and public services were almost non-existent. Taxation was arbitrary and unequal. Order was maintained fitfully, and in the peripheral areas not at all. Within the *Badia*, Bedouin tribes were allowed to continue their traditional *ghazu* as long as they did not encroach on the settled areas. The Ottomans thus maintained a firm but static hold over urban areas, while ignoring the Bedouin disturbances in the countryside. With the exception of some periodic uprisings of local leaders, this routine was the accepted background to the life of the masses. The ruling classes, the military and intellectual elite had little interest in any economic change, let alone the technological advances of the West. Over the centuries, however, European ideas and practices gradually permeated this stagnant system. By the early twentieth century, the whole of the Ottoman Empire had been forced into the political and economic orbit of the West. Northern Arabia was racked by turmoil, and the *Badia*, the traditional retreat of the Bedouin, became a focus of controversy and conflict.

European expansion began in the sixteenth century with French negotiations for an alliance of sorts with the Ottoman Empire. In 1536, the Ottoman Sultan granted French merchants in Ottoman territory certain rights and privileges, called the 'Capitulations'. These essentially permitted the Christian non-Ottoman subject to be judged according to the laws of his own country even while living in Ottoman territory. In the course of the following two centuries, similar grants were made to England (1583), Holland (1613), Austria (1718), Russia (1784) and to almost every other major power, including the United States. At first these concessions were no more than gestures of condescension. They were, to the Ottoman mind, no more than the granting to Europeans of the rights of the *dhimmi* ('the Christian and Jewish protected peoples' tolerated by Islam within Moslem-ruled territory). Once these concessions had been granted, European economic penetration developed rapidly. Trade grew steadily, and numerous colonies of merchants sprang up along the cities on the Mediterranean coastline under the protection of their consuls. Every foreign colony in the Ottoman Empire became, thereby, a state within a state.

Until the close of the eighteenth century, commerce was the primary concern of the mainly French and British merchants and traders. As the century drew to a close, however, relations began to take on political importance. In Egypt, more than in any other Ottoman district, French commercial competition began seriously to undermine local luxury commodities. The native social and economic order became severely strained and restive. Finally, in 1798, Napoleon landed in Egypt, ostensibly to protect the French merchant colony from local misrule. In fact, it was an attempt to create a French base of operations to counter British overseas expansion. Napoleon's presence in Egypt was short-lived, but it marked the beginning of a new period of direct Western intervention in the Arab provinces of the Ottoman Empire. In 1801, the French forces withdrew from Egypt, only to be replaced by the English a little over half a century later. Here again a military incursion was given an economic veneer. Serious financial overextension in the Egyptian province, and the threat of bankruptcy finally culminated in British intervention. At first the Egyptian government was merely forced to accept a system whereby Europe controlled the country's finances. However, when the Egyptian army led a move to replace the Europeans, British forces attacked Alexandria and in 1882 occupied the country.

The nineteenth century saw Europe increasingly concerned with the development and control, one way or another, of the resources and services in the area. Great Britain, for example, ran a regular shipping service from India both to Basra at the mouth of the Persian Gulf and to the Suez. Its naval might was employed to secure these sea routes. Arabian piracy was put down by force of arms along the eastern coast of Arabia, culminating in the peace treaty of 1820 with the Gulf sheikhs. The capture and occupation of Aden in 1839 similarly secured the sea approach to the Suez. With control over the Suez and the Mesopotamian basin firmly established, the British then looked at Northern Arabia as the vital corridor between its two spheres of influence.

The political and economic control that Europe had come to exert in the region was accompanied by a parallel development in cultural and intellectual dominance. This penetration was, at first, religious in character, with each European nation assuming protection over the *dhimmi* (Protected People) community that most closely reflected the religious make-up of its own nation. France, for example, became the protector of Latin Catholicism in Northern Arabia, and Czarist Russia the protector of the Orthodox. As the century wore on, the religious rivalry of the European powers for the protection of the indigenous Christian minorities intensified, and missionary activity became extensive. British missionary activity was relatively small and limited in scope. One hospital and fewer than thirty schools had been established by English, Scottish, and Irish missions. Small local Anglican and Presbyterian communities formed around English churches in the major cities.

French efforts, however, were much more widespread. The Jesuits established and directly maintained important schools, seminaries, and later a university. Franciscans and Lazarists operated several dozen missionary stations. Carmelites, Capuchins, Dominicans, Benedictines, Trappists, and others were also represented throughout the coastline region. With a few notable exceptions (British, American, and Danish), the medical care and hospitalization of the public was chiefly to be found in the hospitals and dispensaries maintained by French Catholic charity and aided by the French government. By the end of the nineteenth century, the French government came to view its achievement along the Mediterranean coastline as incomparable with any other European power. The 'Faith and the Flag' had gained in the Levant, and its wholly 'disinterested and nonacquisitive civilizing mission' had to be continued. Claiming particular gifts for the uplifting of backward peoples, France had, in the nineteenth century, added one territory after another to her colonial empire (Algeria in 1830, Tunis in 1881). There was little doubt in France that the Mediterranean coastline, the 'France of the East', would take its due place beside them (Longrigg).

As France and England carved out their economic, political, and cultural spheres of influence in the Ottoman provinces of Northern Arabia, they also inadvertently fed the flames of popular unrest against the Ottoman Empire. Arab nationalism was slowly gathering strength and would one day seriously challenge the European spheres of influence. In the urban centres of the Ottoman Empire, the Arabs came to be particularly dubious of their future. The 'Young Turk' Revolution of 1908, and the replacement of Islam by Turkism as the basis of the Ottoman Empire, alarmed them.

The majority of these educated Arabs preferred some sort of decentralization of the Empire, perhaps in an Arab-Turkish federation. However, repression of such discussion pushed the activists underground, where they formed secret societies aimed at Arab independence. The outbreak of World War I, which saw Britain and France allied against Germany and the Ottoman Empire, gave these groups an opportunity to act. In 1916, they persuaded the Hashimite *Sharif* (descendant of Hasan, one of the grandsons of Mohammed the Prophet) of Mecca to ally himself with the British and to proclaim an Arab revolt against the Ottoman.

In the arid steppe lands of Central Arabia, a second challenger to the Ottoman Empire and later to the European spheres of influence was gathering force. The Wahhabi movement of two centuries earlier burst into life again, led by Abdul Aziz Al-Saud. This movement had its origins in the general orthodox revivals that had been building since the 1700s in the outlying areas of the Ottoman province. The Sanusi in North Africa, the Mahdists in the Sudan, and the Wahhabi in Central Arabia, among others, were all reform movements that condemned the moral laxity and corruption of Islam under the Ottoman Sultan. Each of these movements aimed to restore the original purity of Islamic organization and faith. They espoused the abolishing of all customary law, and the return to the Koran and *Sunna* (custom associated with Mohammed) as the exclusive sources of Islamic law. The quarrel of these reform movements in the eighteenth and nineteenth centuries had been with other Moslems. By the end of the nineteenth century, however, it included the Western powers. They regarded the European presence in the Arab provinces of the Ottoman Empire as a betrayal of Islam.

Abdul Aziz's revival, however, had a more complicated political and territorial base. A hundred years earlier, the Albanian governor of Egypt, Mohammed Ali, had moved into North and Central Arabia and conquered it. In the process of consolidating his authority, he smashed the Saudi Imamate (1818) in Al-Hasa, deported the family to Egypt, and executed their leader. Subsequent Ottoman control in the region was harsh, and growing numbers of Arab tribal leaders became disenchanted. Gradually they began to unite under various leaders like Abdul Aziz. In 1902 the Al-Saud, under Abdul Aziz's leadership, recaptured Al-Riyadh, their ancestral home. By 1906 the last Ottoman troops had been evicted from Central Arabia, and Abdul Aziz proceeded to establish his hold over much of the territory.

Historians have generally represented the Al-Saud as anti-Ottoman and pro-British during this period. Such a view, as Helms points out, is not absolutely tenable. The religious banner that flew over his military campaigns to re-establish the Al-Saud as a ruling elite in Central Arabia totally opposed any European presence in Arabia. It sought to cleanse and purify the Islamic foundations of the Ottoman Empire rather than separate from it. Evidence seems to suggest that the Al- Saud merely saw Britain as a convenient vehicle to consolidate its political control. In fact, when Great Britain refused to help Abdul Aziz prior to World War I, he began negotiations with the Ottomans (Helms, 1981:117). A treaty was concluded between the Al-Saud and the Ottomans (15 May 1914), but was unratified because of the outbreak of the World War. It contained the Ottoman recognition of Al-Saud's hereditary rights over Al-Hasa. This treaty is clear evidence that Abdul Aziz had little reservation about negotiating with either the British or the Ottoman. His primary concern was to secure his family's right to rule in Central Arabia.

When World War I broke out, Abdul Aziz agreed to support Great Britain against the Ottoman. It was, however, very much a partnership of convenience. The British controlled the eastern coastal city-states of Arabia and were allied with the Hashimite family of Mecca. A long standing rivalry existed between the Al-Saud and the Al-Hashim of the Hijaz that re-emerged in the Arab revolt of 1916. Both the Al- Hashim and the Al-Saud had aspirations of total control over the Arabs, and both saw themselves as leading a cause to free the Arabs and Islam from corrupt forces.

At the close of World War I, Abdul Aziz and his Wahhabi warriors (the *Ikhwan*) constituted a powerful force in Arabia. He was now in a strong position to oppose the Hashimite as well as the British. Eventually he was able to annex the entire Hijaz and send the Al-Hashim into exile. At the same time he clearly demarcated the extent of his territorial claims to Northern Arabia. These demands were to interfere seriously with British and French interests. Abdul Aziz regarded the territories 'as far north as Aleppo and the river Orontes in North Syria [including], the whole country on the river bank of the Euphrates from there down to Basra in the Persian Gulf' as formerly under Al-Saud control, and therefore now his by virtue of his hereditary rights (Helms, 1981:100).

In Europe, more conservative plans were being negotiated. Joint European control had been highly developed in the Ottoman area. And the victors in World War I did not anticipate ending their hegemony. Thus the conquered Ottoman provinces were to be divided according to spheres of influence. The British were to retain Egypt and the Suez Canal, both of which were considered essential to their lines of communication with India. The French were to be granted the northern Mediterranean coastline, where they had special interests growing out of their Catholic missionary work. Iraq and the Persian Gulf, again considered vital for the defence of India, were to be given to Britain. And the *Badia* of Northern Arabia was to be sliced into two, half of which was to go to France, the other half to Great Britain.

The revelation of these plans based on the Sykes-Picot Agreement between France and Great Britain (see map 3) shocked not only the Arabs, but the Americans as well. Both were under the impression that victory in World War I would mean that enduring peace would be established on the basis of self-determination of peoples. The Americans were satisfied, however, when the League of Nations was set up and the spheres of influence in the conquered lands were proclaimed to be temporary means of tutelage. Under mandate from the League of Nations, the French and British would guide the backward people of the former Ottoman Empire to independence.

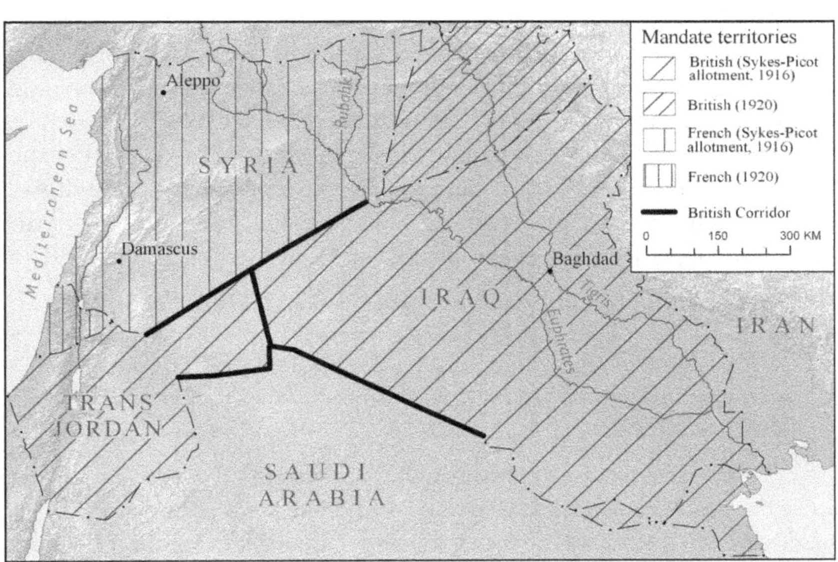

Map 3. Sykes-Picot Allotment
Based on sketch in Longrigg, 1958, p.57

With a shaky hold over their mandated territories, France and Great Britain turned their attention to the creation of borders that would provide them with buffer zones. The French-mandated geographic Syria encompassed the Mediterranean coastline (Lebanon) and the northern *Badia.* The British authority extended over Mesopotamia, the central *Badia*, southern Syria (Palestine), and Trans-Jordan. After intense political negotiations Britain succeeded in installing the sons of the Hashimite *Sharif* of Mecca – Abdullah and Faysal – as rulers of the mandated territories of Trans-Jordan and Iraq. This created an unbroken line of Hashimite rule from the Hijaz north to Jordan and across to Iraq. It assured Britain of a safe network linking the Suez with its Persian Gulf interests. The corridor, nevertheless, sliced through Bedouin territory and in particular the large geographic segment controlled by the Aneza confederation of tribes. The French regarded the corridor with great suspicion and actively supported the efforts of the Bedouin, whose territory it was, to eliminate it. It created a dangerous zone of contention between French interests to the north, British interest to the east and west, and Al-Saud interests in the south.

An artificial grid system of linear borders was agreed upon and established by the mandatory powers. They were designed by the French and British authorities to further their own ends, and only secondary consideration was given to the needs of the local populations. Their main concern was to secure their strategic interests. Territorial border settlements, therefore, were based upon lines that were most advantageous for transportation and communication, even if this sometimes seriously endangered the ability of a state to survive. This policy is well illustrated in a telegram sent to the War Office from British General Headquarters in Mesopotamia in 1919:

> With reference to boundary you are considering along the Khabur [Euphrates tributary]. Being lines of convergence of interests rather than boundaries, rivers are not suitable for frontiers in this country. Line through open desert preferable for a frontier and this would make administration more easy. (Helms, 1981:192)

The drawing of a 'line through open desert', however, could not solve the problem of establishing secure and incontestable boundaries. The desert (*Badia*) simply was not open. It was populated by numerous Bedouin pastoral tribes whose mode of life depended upon seasonal movement from one pasture to another, and access to summer wells and to settled areas. The frontiers of these tribal and trade zones were constantly changing. The new borders proposed to cut through these spheres, separating populations from fundamental elements in their economic, commercial, and social universe.

To the south, British mandate authorities concerned themselves with defining the borders between those of the autonomous ruler Abdul Aziz Al-Saud and their Hashimite states. Abdul Aziz never concealed his hatred of the Hashimite kings, Abdullah and Faysal, and persisted in trying to erode their control in Trans-Jordan and Iraq. He refused to accept the fixed borders arbitrarily determined by the mandate powers claiming, correctly, that they were unsuitable for pastoral nomadic life. A more local political principle, however, underpinned his argument. If the allegiance of a tribe could be secured, then rights to the tribe's territory could be claimed. In this way, he could continue to extend his authority by inducing tribes to pledge allegiance to him. Thus, the negotiations between Abdul Aziz and the British were long and drawn out. And not an inch of border along the entire circumference of what came to be recognized as the Kingdom of Saudi Arabia was uncontested (Helms).

To the north, along the French-mandated territory of the Mediterranean coast and the northern *Badia,* different concerns were paramount. Unlike the southern portions, this region encompassed highly developed urban centres, rich agrarian communities, and extensive tribal associations, all mutually dependent upon one another. The creation of national borders significantly disturbed the population, especially as the territory had become a haven for refugees from other parts of the former Ottoman province. Serious difficulties developed as the French tried to administer and pacify this dislocated population. Within the borders of the mandated territory, the French drew a line following the frontiers of agriculture. In this sphere, modern French administration was to reign. Beyond it, in the *Badia,* an entirely separate system of control and administration developed, which was to seriously impinge upon the future integration of the Bedouin tribes in the nation-state.

PACIFICATION OF THE BEDOUIN

Perhaps no error in policy was more persistent than the French refusal to recognize the essential unity of Greater Syria. In their mandate, the French sought to increase their strength by following a policy of 'divide and rule'. Thus they explicitly supported all religious minorities in an effort to weaken the nascent Arab nationalist movement. France created the predominantly Christian country of Lebanon by uniting the old Ottoman province of Mount Lebanon with the coastal cities of Tripoli, Beirut, Sidon, and Tyre, and the predominantly Moslem plain of the Bekaa. The rest of the territory was divided into five semi-dependent parts accentuating religious differences and cultivating regional as against national sentiment (e.g., Jebel Druze, Aleppo, Latakia, Damascus, and Alexandretta). The Druze were given a separate administration on the Jebel Druze. The northern coastline and the Jebel Al-Nasariyyah, an Alawite stronghold, were united into the state of Latakia. Further north, the district of Alexandretta (Hatay Turkey) with a sizable Turkish minority was given its own government. The Bedouin in the *Badia* were separated out and encouraged to set up their own nation supervised by a special French unit, the Contrôle Bedouin. This semi-autonomous department

> managed over the following decades, by its posts, patrols, and mechanized armament to maintain good order in the desert. Taxation of the tribesmen was rebased, their direct representation in the chamber assured their quarrels compromised, their arms controlled, desert wells dug, seasonal mid-desert schools opened, and mobile health clinics [set up]. (Longrigg, 1958: 283)

These well-meant measures could scarcely survive the mandate. In some ways this policy worked to the detriment of the future of the Bedouin. By separating them physically and administratively from the rest of the country and giving them a special status, the French served only to underscore the unsympathetic, if not contemptuous, attitude of the intelligentsia and Arab officialdom to Bedouin pastoral life and needs. French interests in creating the Contrôle Bedouin had more concrete foundations than simple romanticism towards the Bedouin. They needed them for a particular reason. French authorities obviously could not leave two-thirds of the mandate territory (the *Badia*) out of their control. They needed to guarantee a continuous and safe passage through the region for commerce and travel to Baghdad. Furthermore, the petroleum line to Mosul had to be secured. The French had two options before them. They could either pacify the area by force of arms or they could 'buy' the support of the tribes by catering to their leaders. Both approaches were attempted at the same time with a number of unexpected results.

With the political fragmentation of geographic Syria into a number of small, non-viable states, there followed numerous population shifts and general discontent among the agricultural and pastoral populations alike. The cession of Cilicia to Turkey drove thousands of Armenians into Syria. The stillbirth of the Treaty of Sèvres (1920) increased the emigration of Kurdish communities from Iraq and Turkey. The installation of the Maronite-oriented state of Lebanon drew increasing numbers of Druze families to the Jebel Druze.

Mass migrations of tribes were also occurring. After Abdul Aziz's success in spreading Wahhabi rule and defeating the Shammar capital of Hail in the *Nejd*, 40,000 Shammar tents left *en masse* and took refuge in the northern *Badia* and in Iraq. At the same time, Aneza and other Bedouin tribal sections, either by attraction to Abdul Aziz's movement, or through disaffection for the French mandate, immigrated to Central Arabia. These included sections of Al-Ruwalla, Al-Hassanna, Fed'aan, Sbaa', and Mawali.

The dislocation of the population was, therefore, a fundamental problem facing the French mandatory authorities upon their arrival. The settlement of Armenian, Kurdish, and later Assyrian and Catholic refugees was a substantial duty of the mandatory power. Refugees were collected from all the territory and systematically settled in predominantly pastoral regions along the borders of the *Badia*, and on marginal land in the Mediterranean coastline.

Once the basic measures for resettlement had been dealt with, the French mandatory authorities were able to concentrate their efforts on the problem of pacification of the country as a whole. Full military occupation in 1919 along the coastal zone had been delayed not only by Turkish resistance, but also by poor communication. Elsewhere, resistance was widespread, especially in relatively inaccessible mountain areas and in the south. Only after two years of military operations was pacification in most areas effected, and the French turned their attention to the control of the *Badia*, home of the Bedouin.

The effort to impose order in this pastoral region could not be implemented until the first camel corps (Méhariste) of the French military was developed. In 1920, a special Bedouin policy was declared placing the Contrôle Bedouin directly under the supervision of the French Délégué at Damascus (Rapport, 1925). French policy here, like the previous Ottoman authority, was limited to trying to maintain a degree of security on the settled margin. The Bedouin were encouraged to conduct their affairs in their traditional manner as long as they did not disturb the settled populations.

During this early period, the French merely requested that the Bedouin not carry arms in settled regions and that, when fighting among themselves, they leave the settled communities in peace. These requests were not respected. In 1921, the first Méhariste outpost established at Deir-ez-Zor was attacked by forces of the Ageidat Bedouin. In the Aleppo district, Bedouin tribes clashed with the newly settled Kurdish and Turkish populations. The perpetually feuding Mawali and Haddiddiin, in a series of intense *ghazu* in the Homs-Hama district, cut the railway line. Finally a French Méhariste column arrived to discipline these tribes in an operation of unusual violence. Several winter tribal settlements were burned, flocks dispersed, and large numbers of people killed (Glubb, 1942). Despite the severity of French retaliation, these two tribes were fighting each other again two years later.

A financial-political understanding between the French authorities and some of the Bedouin tribal leaders (e.g., Emir Faour Al-Faour of Al-Fadl, Trad-il-Milhem of Al- Hassanna, and Nuri Sha'laan of Al-Ruwalla) resulted in greater French tolerance over the next few years of the occasional skirmish and raid (Al-Faour, 1968; Glubb, 1942; Oppenheim, 1939). With the outbreak of the Druze Revolt between 1925 and 1927, the well-justified fear of tribal participation brought about an abrupt change in the French policy towards the Bedouin.

As the Druze revolt spread out from the Hauran over most of the mandate territory, sympathetic Bedouin tribes increased their raiding activities. In the Homs-Hama region, for example, the Haddiddiin tribe attacked and pillaged Hama, cutting communications and destroying much government property. French authority was only restored two days later when air bombardments and emergency forces were put into action. The following spring the Haddiddiin and some Mawali tribes were again bombarded while returning from their winter migrations to the Homs-Hama region. Fearing renewed tribal agitation in the area of Aleppo, Homs, and Hama, the French actively sought to bomb the tribes before they could do any damage (Rapport, 1925).

The use of air bombardments against the tribes naturally guaranteed a peaceful spring in the Homs-Hama pasture areas. It was also the first indicator of a new aggressive and highly successful policy towards the Bedouin. Raiding, even when only between tribes, was actively suppressed by modern arms. Finally, in 1927, the French authorities convened an 'assembly' of sheikhs at Hama in order to effect a reconciliation between the tribes that would end tribal hostility and threats to local security. This assembly in itself was not enough to end the hostility between competitive tribes. The French therefore decided to supplement these imposed peace treaties with the payment of monthly subsidies to each tribal leader. These subsidies, not unlike *khuwa* payments in the eyes of the Bedouin, strengthened and consolidated the relative authority and prestige of individual leaders in the eyes of the Bedouin population. At the close of this conference, a peace was concluded between the Haddiddiin and Mawali, Al-Ruwalla and Sbaa', the Faware (Al-Fadl) and the Beni Khalid, and the Fed'aan and the Shammar.

Despite the Conference of 1925, hostilities between the Shammar and Aneza confederacies continues to disturb the region. In 1930 a new conference was assembled at Palmyra. The French tried to adjudicate the rift that threatened to split the Aneza confederation into two warring factions. Besides imposing a settlement, the French added new regulations and services. They established a system of crime control that formally placed all affairs in the pastoral zone not under the jurisdiction of the sheikhs alone, but equally with the Contrôle Bedouin. Affairs that involved individuals in the cultivated zone were placed under the jurisdiction of the ordinary tribunal. To sweeten this reduction in the sheikhs' authority, the French began a program to build new wells and restore old *qanats* (underground water systems), to increase the number of mobile schools and the number of mobile clinics (Rapport, 1930; 1931). Many of the tribes refused to accept the subordination to the Contrôle that these efforts implied. Some sections of tribes broke away from the main body and sought refuge with other tribes beyond the borders of the French Mandate. Sections of the Al-Ruwalla, for example, under the leadership of Farhan-il-Meshhour, left the Damascus region with 1,000 tents and joined the forces of Abdul Aziz Al-Saud. Others, like the Wuld Sliman, broke away from the Fed'aan and returned to Central Arabia as did sections of the Ageidat.

The numerous sheikhs' assemblies at Deir-ez-Zor, Hama, and Palmyra, the paying of subsidies to select tribal leaders, and the departure of recalcitrant tribal units, marked the complete takeover by the Contrôle Bedouin as a supervisory body in charge of Bedouin affairs. As such, they effectively 'froze' the social situation. They recognized the tribal sheikhs that they would deal with and, in doing so, slowly robbed them of their popular base of support. The monthly subsidies rendered the sheikhs 'powerless elites'. Technically they had little formal responsibility vis-a-vis their tribal members. The French had taken over, arresting once-fluid social and physical universes for better administrative purposes. Tribal rights to particular pasture areas and watering places were recognized and patrolled by the French. Effective control over the ban on carrying arms in settled regions was established, and payment of taxes (in lump sums) was rigidly enforced.

In return, the tribal leaders were granted automatic representation in the National Assembly (many of these tribal leaders, in a resurgence of political strength after Independence, were to return as elected members of Parliament), and their requests for development assistance were heard, if not frequently carried out. The French had, in effect, smashed the political power of the Bedouin tribal leaders and were now dealing with them as they would any rural or urban political leader.

During this period, the British were having similar problems with Bedouin tribes. Theirs, however, was a highly complex situation that revolved around the issue of fixed boundaries. By 1926, Abdul Aziz had consolidated his control over Central Arabia and the Hijaz and was actively engaged in eroding Hashimite control in Trans-Jordan and Iraq. The British pressed Abdul Aziz to accept fixed boundaries between these British-mandated kingdoms and his state. Aware of the problems of nomadic pastoralism, Abdul Aziz objected to frontiers based on territorial rather than tribal lines. He, therefore, procrastinated in all treaty negotiations, and at the same time encouraged his Wahhabi *Ikhwan* to raid and 'convert' tribes on that frontier.

A unique situation developed when the Bedouin tribes that moved along these frontiers realized that they could take advantage of the new mandate system by freely raiding one another and then escaping into the territory of another leader. A typical example of this actively developed along the southern Iraqi frontier. *Ikhwan* raids had resulted in many tribes, particularly the Shammar, seeking refuge in Iraq, or with the Amarat Aneza in the *Badia*. Bedouin tradition prescribes that anyone asking for protection, even an enemy, is entitled to receive it. Furthermore, any tribe under protection, is not permitted to continue its hostilities while under that protection. Thus the Shammar were received by the Amarat Aneza. A major conflict arose, however, when the Shammar began to use the Amarat territory as a base for their counter-raids against Abdul Aziz. When Abdul Aziz responded by demanding that the Shammar be returned to him for punishment, the British ordered the Shammar away from the frontier, and well under their surveillance. British-mandated Iraq continued to house the Shammar, but was unable to prevent them from conducting violent raids against Abdul Aziz and his *Ikhwan*. Finally Abdul Aziz called for their expulsion and claimed that his authority over this tribe transcended state boundaries. The British in Iraq refused his demand, claiming the right, by Bedouin custom, not to return criminals who sought refuge in their territory. Thus, when the British pressured Abdul Aziz to stop the *Ikhwan* raids along the frontier, he maintained that he could hardly regain control of those guilty of raiding if they were assured of asylum in Iraq.

As the ferocity of the *Ikhwan* raids grew, the British became seriously concerned. They feared that this instability would lead to the defection or 'conversion' of many of the Iraqi-based tribes, as it already had in Trans-Jordan among the Howeitat. Segments of the Aneza in French-controlled territory were threatening to join the *Ikhwan* for their own protection if these raids could not be stopped. Finding it increasingly difficult to defend the long frontier from raids, the British called out the Royal Air Force. Aerial bombings of large magnitude were carried out as a deterrent against the raiding tribes. Abdul Aziz strongly protested the British bombing of tribes who were supposed to be guilty of raiding. He also challenged what he saw as a double standard. While he was not allowed to punish raiders who escaped into Iraq, Britain felt justified in crossing over into his territory and bombing his subjects. In a letter to the Political Agent in Bahrain, he referred to 'the action ... that the British Government intend to send their aeroplanes into the interior of our country for the punishment of our subjects. This ... is a new principle which no government law will accept.' (Helms, 1981:235) Abdul Aziz was not under any mandate authority. He was an autonomous Arab leader of an independent state. Yet the British, when unable to convince him of the 'correctness' of European logic, resorted to dealing with him by force of arms. After nearly a decade of opposing the imposition of fixed Western-style boundaries that restricted his own authority, Abdul Aziz and his Bedouin-based *Ikhwan* had no choice but to submit.

The outstanding power of the modern state, as Gellner points out (Nelson, ed., 1973), leaves little room for surprise at the consequent adaptation of pastoralists along economic rather than political lines. The state currently is the overwhelming power and the pastoral communities being studied today have as their context the modern state with its technologically advanced military force. Thus, the model set up by Ibn Khaldun – of opposition between two relatively balanced forces, central authority and tribal authority, and cyclical swings from one to the other throughout history – no longer holds in the twentieth century. The retreat of the Bedouin is no longer possible, as he cannot get out of the reach of central authority. He has no choice but to begin to transform his political strength into economic strength. In many ways the same developments instrumental in robbing the Bedouin tribes of their political might, the development of rapid transport and the introduction of motor vehicles, were, eventually, to be used by these populations as a basis for new economic power.

With a system of security firmly established in geographic Syria, the French-mandate authorities turned their attention to the development of a national infrastructure. The slow pace of early manoeuvres and the peculiar mobility of their adversaries emphasized to the mandatory powers the urgency of an effective road and communication system. A telegraph and road network was developed, linking the country in a system more advanced than any found in any neighbouring mandate territory. In 1920, with a population of approximately 2.5 million, French reports estimate that 700 kilometres of roads existed (Rapport, 1923, 1924). By 1940, with a population of around 4.5 million, there were 2,900 kilometres of roads (Rapport, 1939, *Statistical Abstract of Syria*, 1951, 1952). During this period, the number of cars increased from 100 to 11,000 (Rapport 1930; 1938). As the network of roads improved, cars began to replace pack animals as a means of transport between city and village.

In the *Badia* the car was not immediately adopted for general transport. The expense necessary to own a car limited its use to very special occasions mainly by the tribal sheikhly elite. And at first the car was enthusiastically adopted by the tribes for *ghazu*. In 1926, for example, Nuri Sha'laan of Al-Ruwalla outfitted three cars with machine guns and one twelve-seater vehicle – ostensibly for pasture reconnaissance but actually for military conveyance. Recognising the real purpose of these vehicles, Sheikh Mejhim of the Fed'aan protested to the French authorities that these vehicles threatened to disturb the balance between the tribes. Thereafter, the French carefully controlled the purchase and utilisation of motor vehicles in the *Badia*. Although the potential of motor transport was recognized early on by the Bedouin, it was going to take more than a simple mechanical device to revive their former strength. The added element, which the French indirectly provided them, was in the realm of land registration and ownership, perhaps the most important infrastructural achievement of the Inter-War Mandate for the country as a whole. In 1923, the French undertook a survey and registration of the entire territory. This development was later to establish rights of ownership, consolidate viable land holdings, and provide a basis for land taxation. By 1930, a new land code and system of title was instituted to replace the centuries-old Ottoman system.

In the sphere of pastoral communities, grazing land traditionally held by the tribe communally came to be registered in the name of an individual, usually a tribal leader. Several tribes, among them Al-Fadl and the Fed'aan, had registered land in the name of their leaders during the Ottoman period. But most tribal territory, including that of Al- Ruwalla and Al-Hassanna, was registered only under the French mandate. In the Homs-Hama region, land encompassing twenty villages was registered in the name of Sheikh Trad il-Milhem of Al-Hassanna. In addition, unregistered land (state land) east of the frontier of cultivation was assigned to tribal authorities by 'emergency decrees' in 1940 and 1941. This emergency legislation granted tribal leaders title to vast expanses of land. In this manner, the Shammar registered in the names of their tribal leaders over 2 million hectares of land in the *Jezireh*. The change from tribal usufruct to individual ownership was to have wide implications upon the total organization of the tribes once these resources were utilized. That was not long in coming, and by the late 1920s associations of city merchants and tribal leaders began to take place. As French supervision of agricultural and pastoral relations became better established, city merchants, especially in Aleppo, began to invest large amounts of money in cultivation. Partnerships were formed between the entrepreneurs and tribal leaders. Typically, under such agreements, the city merchants supplying mechanized equipment, seeds, and labour, were able to open vast tracts of land previously uncultivated in tribal areas of the *Jezireh*. In return for this right of cultivation a certain percentage of the crop or profit (from 10 to 15 per cent) was granted to the tribal leaders.

After the 1940–41 emergency decrees, this method of exploitation was assured even greater success. The *Jezireh*, previously classified as state domain and restricted from agricultural exploitation was now officially registered in the name of tribal leaders. Very large areas of uncultivated lands were leased to the 'tractor-entrepreneurs' for mechanized cultivation and grain production. This rapid agricultural push at the expense of grazing land had numerous effects on the different Bedouin tribes. In the 1920s a number of tribal groups had left the mandate territory to remove themselves from the political sphere of influence of the French. In 1938, the Contrôle Bedouin reported that, as a result of the agricultural expansion, large numbers of the Aneza confederation from Al-Hassanna, Al-Ruwalla, Sbaa', and Fed'aan were leaving the territory and remaining in Central Arabia (Rapport, 1938).

The steady process of extending cultivated land was met in two ways by the tribes who remained on their traditional pasture land. Some tribal units began cultivating land, making token presentations or rental payments to their leaders each year. Other tribal units began to reduce the extent of their migration and ration grazing in the face of diminishing pasture land. A third option, reported by the early 1930s in French studies, was the growing phenomenon whereby camel raising, as it became less lucrative, was progressively abandoned for sheep raising, not only along the frontiers of cultivation but within the *Badia* itself (Rapport, 1931). Some of the Bedouin, like the Al-Ruwalla, who had turned to sheep raising, began to push farther out into the *Badia* in their seasonal migrations. With the network of roads well developed, these tribes were able to use water trucks to bring water to their herds instead of relying only on local ground water or wells. Thus a modern form of animal husbandry was developing, whereby sheep could be maintained in areas not previously usable.

Still other tribes or tribal sections, such as the Fadl and the Hassanna, moved deeper into agricultural regions in their seasonal migrations, utilizing marginal areas within the Mediterranean coastline. Attempting to adapt their life mode to the human and physical environment, these tribal sections adopted increasingly sedentary residences and combined their pastoral activities with *secondary* concerns, such as farming, commerce, and seasonal labour.

The French-Mandate policy and the infrastructure they developed were key factors in the rapid national economic growth after independence. However, their policy of 'divide and rule' in general, and the separate and special status they gave the Bedouin tribes, did not help the Bedouin cause after independence. If the French mandatory authority had planned to create a separate pastoral nation, as some Contrôle Bedouin officers seem to have attempted in 1937 (Hourani, 1946), the independent government wanted only to integrate all elements of the country into a single united whole

~ 3 ~

Arab Society and the Bedouin

The Middle East has been called by many a patchwork or 'mosaic' of cultures. Its ecologically based pastoral, agrarian, and urban communities intermingle with numerous ethnic, religious, and linguistic associations of peoples. These various peoples, when taken as a whole, form what is commonly referred to as 'Arab society'. The Bedouin of Northern Arabia are but one component of this composite whole. Too often, however, the distinctiveness of the Bedouin, as well as other peoples, is stressed, while the wholeness of the society is passed over. Yet there are threads holding these separate units together. These bonds are fundamental patterns of behaviour that have developed over centuries in response to common historical and ecological constraints. Each unit accentuates or de-emphasizes behaviour norms to adapt to the demands of its immediate universe. Thus, the Bedouin can best be understood first by exploring some of the shared patterns of behaviour in Arab society, and second by examining how these norms operate in the pastoral nomadic society of Northern Arabia today.

The fundamental unit of organization in any society is the family. Given the heterogeneity of peoples encompassed by the term 'Arab society', can one speak of **the** Arab family? To do so is to ignore certain differences between urban and rural areas, skilled and unskilled workers, and of course Moslems and Christians. One can perhaps discuss the Moslem family in general despite these differences, because as a model it displays certain patterns common throughout the whole of Arab society. Over the centuries, Islam and its prescriptions for family life have influenced and, at times, limited the extent of variation in family behaviour norms. Ecological and historical factors have also operated in various communities to refine, and conversely to cloud, certain details. Thus among the pastoral nomadic Bedouin tribes in Northern Arabia, particular features of the Arab family stand in clear relief, while others are obscured.

In all Arab communities, life pivots around the family. The individual's loyalty to it is nearly absolute and generally overrides all other obligations.

Except in more westernized urban circles, the individual's standing as a social being depends on his family background. To ask an Arab where he is from usually draws a response not of geographical region, but of family origin. Among the Bedouin, both kinship and territory are encompassed by the response of tribal affiliation. The individual's attitude, his loyalty to his kin group, his obligations and rights in the life of the community, and his political and social attachments are vividly illustrated in this widespread Bedouin Arab saying:

> I against my brothers
> I and my brothers against my cousins
> I and my brothers and my cousins against the world.

In the West, it is the individual who can act and accomplish tasks alone, whereas, in Arab society, activity requires the support of a group – generally the kin group – in economic, social, and political affairs. Alone, there is peril, while as a group there is support and refuge.

In urban areas, ingrained feelings of duty towards a job, an employer, or even a friend are not prevalent. The Arab saying quoted above attests to the widespread conviction that the only reliable people are one's kinsmen. Thus, an office holder tends to select his kinsmen as fellow workers not only because of a sense of responsibility for them, but also because of the feeling of trust between them. Commercial establishments are largely family operations staffed by cousins or nephews of the owner. And cooperation among traditional and some modern business firms may be determined by the presence or absence of kinship ties between the heads of firms. There is no basis for a close relationship except kinship.

The structure of the Arab family, Moslem or Christian, is basically the same as that of the Western family, but the former has changed less. As in the West, descent is reckoned through the males, and the Arab father is the head of the family; the Arab father, however, exercises greater authority.

In a community, family solidarity is highly valued, and consequently so too is the obedience of children. In the three-generation household, it is the senior generation that is in charge. The father is the head of the home, and the mother is the supervisor of the household. Even in the more recent two-generation household, obedience is still stressed, and grown children are respectful and submissive to parents into adulthood, whether living in the same household or not. In fact it is not uncommon for men in their thirties or forties to show subservience to their elders. Very often the West-

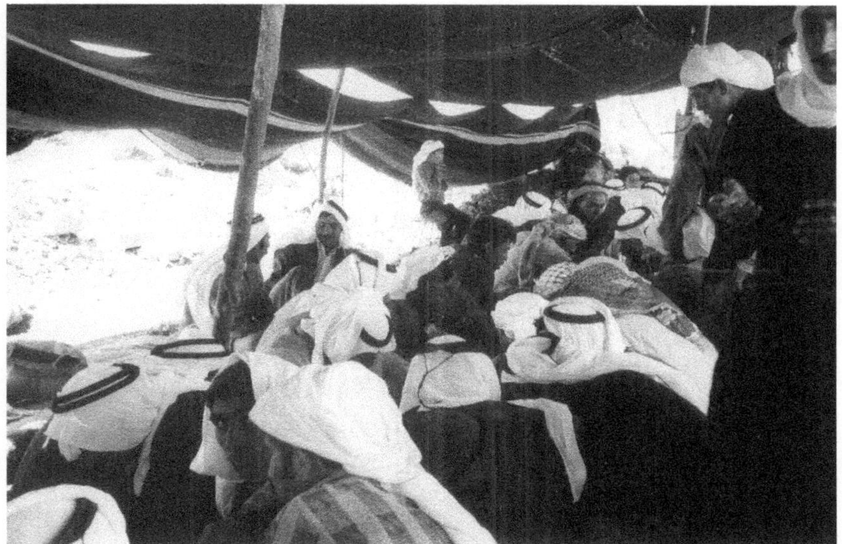

Dawn Chatty

Plate 4. Close-up of male guests eating at a wedding (Al-Fadl)

erner mistakenly expects the most 'educated' or 'Westernized' individual in a family to be the decision-maker, where in fact it is the oldest who holds that special role.

Individual families form larger units (minimal lineages) based on patrilineal descent from a common ancestor. In cities, villages, and tribes, these units are the basic organizing divisions. They maintain a corporate identity in tribal and village affairs. In urban centres they often constitute residential neighbourhoods or quarters. These minimal lineages are recognized by the names of their founding ancestor and are called *Beits* (extended family or lineage).[1] In tribal society (e.g., the Bedouin, the Druze, the Alawite, the Kurds, the Turkman) these *Beits* form the basis for wider forms of economic, social, and political organizations – the *qabila* (tribe).

The most significant independent unit within the tribal kinship system is the *khamsa*. This is a group of patrilateral male relatives, which identifies itself by its blood relationship to a direct forebear. Thus, taking

1. *Beit* (meaning minimal lineage) appears in the text in upper case so as to differentiate it from *beit* (meaning house or tent), which is in lower case.

the grandfather, for example, 'ego', brothers, father, uncles, and uncles' sons form a *khamsa.* It is within this unit, especially in the past when cases of homicide-vengeance were common, that security needs were highly significant. Outside this unit, the individual's possessions, his family, and his very life were, or could be, exposed to danger. Within this unit, there was safety. These blood-ties were the basis of actual cooperation and mutual aid in danger. Even today this unit is operative, especially among some Bedouin, Druze, Kurdish, and Alawite communities.

Blood-ties were – and, to some extent, still are – as important in urban centres as among tribal communities. Many quarters in Arab cities like Baghdad, Aleppo, Homs, Damascus, and Amman were formed around kin groups. Until recently, in Damascus, for example, whole *harahs* (residential quarters) were owned by a family (e.g., Azem, Halbouni, Midani, Qudsi, Mahayni, Quwatli). In each of these cities, major families formed important residential, social, economic, and political units.

Marriage in Arab society is very much a union between two families, not two individuals. Ideally one should marry within the lineage. Parallel cousins, or the children of two brothers are considered the most appropriate mates. This is particularly true among the Bedouin, where *ibn amm* (son of father's brother) or *bint amm* (daughter of father's brother) marriages are frequent. In other regions, particularly in villages throughout the country, the *ibn amm* has first priority to marry the *bint amm.* In the major urban centres, however, the custom is breaking down, especially among the middle classes. Often the wealthy marry within their family to keep property holdings within the lineage, while the poor do so to lower the *mahr* (bride wealth payment) made by a man to the bride and her family. *Mahr* fluctuates tremendously in relationship to the social positions of the families. In cities along the Mediterranean coastline, this generally runs to approximately four to five thousand dollars. Among the Bedouin in Northern Arabia, ten to twelve thousand dollars is not uncommon. In the oil-rich states of Saudi Arabia and the Gulf, even higher figures are known. In Arab society, husband and wife usually call each other *ibn ammi* or *bint ammi* (son or daughter of my father's brother), even though they may not be so related.

Marriage between first cousins is common among the Druze, Kurds and Turkman. It is forbidden among the Circassians and Christians. Even so, groups that forbid marriage of first cousins encourage the marriage of more distant cousins, and thereby generally preserve a lineage endogamy.

Dawn Chatty

Plate 5. A wedding celebration in Bekka Valley of Lebanon (Al-Fadl)

Marriage is thus viewed as a practical bond between families and often has political and economic overtones even among the poorer people.

Though still permitted, polygamy is declining, especially in cities but also in villages and among pastoral tribes. The rising educational levels of both men and women, economic changes, legal changes, and new moral and religious ideas are bringing forth a society in which polygamy today is accounted for by men with only two wives. Among the Bedouin, most cases of polygamy are ones in which the first wife proved barren, and, rather than divorce her, a second wife is taken to bear children.

The rules of divorce in Arab Moslem society have until recently been governed exclusively by the *Koran* (2:226–38), which, like the Old Testament, gives only men the right to dissolve a marriage. The husband, until recently, dissolved the marriage merely by saying to his wife three times, in the presence of witnesses, 'I divorce you'. In so doing, he was required to complete the second portion of the *mahr* (usually two-thirds of the total) that he had not been obliged to pay at the time of the marriage. A divorced

Dawn Chatty

Plate 6. Male guests at wedding (Al-Fadl)

wife was returned to her father's family and usually found little difficulty in marrying again. In fact, a married woman's ties with her own parental kinsmen are never weakened. As a wife, she is expected to support her husband and his family, but as a daughter she maintains the moral support of her father and brothers. Often she will put their interests before those of her husband. Furthermore, her father's household always remains open to her, and, in case of a dispute with her husband, she returns to her father's house. This occurs frequently in most urban, rural, and tribal areas.

Traditionally a woman could obtain a divorce from her husband only by going to a religious court and demanding that the judge require her husband to divorce her. More recently, women have taken to writing specific terms in their marriage contracts regarding their right to divorce or their husbands' right to take additional wives. Also, the institution of *mahr* required to conclude a marriage contract, of which two-thirds is held by the groom to be transferred to the bride in case of death or divorce, serves to act as a brake against hasty divorce.

Inheritance and succession in Arab society are handled in much the same manner as descent. Important property holdings and positions of leadership are passed down within the lineage patrilaterally, from one male paternal kinsman to another. Inheritance of all forms of property among Moslems is governed by the detailed rules set forth in the *Koran* (4:12). A Moslem may, in his will, freely dispose of only one-third of his property; the remainder must be distributed in accordance with Koranic prescriptions. Sons inherit equally, each one receiving twice as much as a daughter. A daughter who is an only child inherits half the property. A wife inherits a quarter if there are no children, but only an eighth if there are children to share the legacy. In general, a woman, when holding title to land, passes it on to her brothers to control in exchange for the security they provide her in time of need.

The high value Arabs place on family solidarity, the respect and obedience accorded family elders, the strong bonds for mutual self-help and cooperation within a tight group of kinsmen are traditional patterns of association still very prevalent among most of the various communities that make up Arab society. The family still serves as a form of elementary social security. It provides welfare assistance to its members, refuge to its women, and a home for its elderly. Educational opportunities by agnatic sponsorship (*khamsa*) of its promising youth is quite common, especially among the Druze and the Kurds. Employment opportunities through its wide kinship and *wastah* network are common throughout the population. The family in Arab society today still maintains a united front in the face of external danger or peril.

MALE AND FEMALE ROLES

The roles of men and women in Arab society can best be described as dichotomous in nature. There is a public and a private world. The public, formal world is very much the stage for men, while the private, informal world is the stage for women. The boundaries between these two spheres, however, do not always fall into Western categories of public and private, where the home or house of the nuclear family is the private sphere, and everything else becomes public domain. So often, a Western visitor, while strolling through an old quarter of an Arab city, will come across men dressed in what appear to be (and are) pyjamas. The first reaction is one of uncomfortable surprise. Gradually the realization comes that these men are not 'in public'. They are within the domain of their family or neighbourhood residence. It is the visitor who, without realizing, has left the public sphere and stumbled on the private and informal world of the Arab.

In Arab society, the 'private' sphere encompasses not only the extended family household, but at times, includes the family neighbourhood in cities and sections of villages in rural areas or, as among the Bedouin, an entire camping area. The critical point is the presence or absence of strangers. For example, among the Bedouin, the women's 'private' sphere extends over the entire camp, where only kin are present. The appearance of a stranger closes up the sphere, and the women withdraw into the folds of their smaller universe in the tent. To the stranger, it appears as though women are either not present or are being secluded in another section of the tent or camp. Frequent visitors to a Bedouin camp, such as itinerant traders or merchants are often addressed in kinship terms like '*akhi*' (my brother) or '*ammi*' (my uncle). Thus, they are temporarily brought into the fold of the private sphere and thereby do not interfere with the regular flow of women's daily work.

In the public sphere, male and female worlds are strictly separated. Men and women seek friendship, amusement, and entertainment with their own sex. Contact between the two sexes takes place primarily within the

Dawn Chatty

Plate 7. Woman milking sheep (Al-Hassanna)

private sphere of the home or neighbourhood. This, however, should not be taken to mean that the women's contribution to the economic, social, or political well-being of the kin group and family is inferior to men's. In rural and tribal areas, women contribute equally on a complementary basis to the group well-being. Roles are strictly divided, and there is very little crossover of duties. In agricultural areas, women carry out at least half, if not more, of the burden of agricultural work in the field as well as the work in the home. In pastoral societies, women own and have financial responsibility for the home or tent. In addition, they milk the herds of sheep and goat daily, while the men who own the flocks are responsible for herding them. In urban centres, where women have been traditionally more secluded, their present role is difficult to assess. No recent studies of any value are available, but the high level of female presence in the urban labour force, government offices, police force, the army, and in secondary schools and universities indicates that profound changes are taking place.

A limited number of traits characteristic to the Arabs, in all their variety, can be inferred from the patterns of behaviour outlined above. These are the concepts of honour and shame and those of hospitality and hostility. Although their development has been affected by numerous ecological and historical factors, the influence of Bedouin and Islamic values is particularly pronounced.

Honour and Shame

On a small scale, exclusive communities that make up Arab society in the face to face, as opposed to anonymous, relations are of paramount importance. Thus, the concepts of honour and shame are the constant preoccupation of individuals. Honour or *sharaf*, which is inherited from the family, has to be constantly asserted and vindicated. A man's share of honour, therefore, is largely determined by his own behaviour and the behaviour of his kinsmen, particularly his near agnatic kin. *Sharaf* can thus be described as honour that is acquired either by personal achievement or through belonging to a certain kin group. In this sense *sharaf* can be subject to increase or decrease, to development or deterioration, according to the conduct of the person and his kin. For women of a kin group or family, there is an exclusive term for their honour, *ird*, used only in connection with female chastity. Women, thus can, and do, play a conspicuous role in determining the honour of a family and lineage in a unique and decisive way that cannot be ignored or minimised. *Ird* differs from *sharaf* in that *sharaf* can be acquired or augmented through right behaviour and achievement, whereas *ird* can only be lost by the 'misconduct' of the woman, and, once lost, it cannot be regained. In many respects, the total honour of a family depends largely on the *ird* of their women. Consequently the conduct of women is expected to be circumspect and modest, and their virtue above reproach. The slightest rumour of a woman's misconduct can irreparably damage the honour of the family. Thus, female virginity before marriage and sexual purity afterwards are essential to the maintenance of family honour. The institution of seclusion and veiling can, therefore, be seen as an attempt to preserve family honour especially in highly populated areas full of non-kinsmen. Veiling is not practiced in villages or tribes, where strict rules for the behaviour of one sex towards another are universally respected and deviants seriously punished.

Hospitality and Hostility: Egotism and Conformity

The Arab seems to hold two major contradictory impulses: egotism and conformity. The first takes the form of extreme self-assertiveness before others. The second takes the shape of obedience to certain group norms. The very nature of human relations in Arab society encourages this paradox. Individual rivalry is itself engendered by the values of the groups to which one owes allegiance. Each individual generally belongs to several such groups, such as, the family, the lineage, the tribe and the religious and ethnic community. Each of these groups has a fierce sense of self-identity, and of difference from others. Yet none of them is able to command enough loyalty to preclude the hostility of the smaller groups within it.

What happens when two exaggerated egos meet? They either clash or find some mode of accommodation. These are the extremes of Arab interpersonal relations: excessive hostility alternating with extreme politeness. Politeness and hospitality are Bedouin virtues extolled by Arabs long before the rise of Islam. In the *Badia*, hospitality comes about as a means of overcoming the individual's helplessness in a harsh environment. The extension of hospitality to a traveller implies reciprocity at some later time. In villages and cities, a different function has come to be added to this pattern of behaviour. Here it serves to control ever-present hostility and keep it from bursting into violence. Exaggerated hospitality and politeness are, at least in part, reactions to excessive hostility.

Dawn Chatty

Plate 8. Man pouring coffee for guests (Al-Hassanna)

Arab life is filled with interpersonal rivalry, tribal feuds in the *Badia,* family and village quarrels in settled regions, and intergroup hostility in urban areas. Politeness is a means of maintaining enough distance to prevent aggressive tendencies from becoming actual. Hospitality and generosity are means of demonstrating friendliness while warding off expected aggression. Such measures as excessive politeness (a form of avoidance) or hospitality (a form of ingratiation in a situation where intimacy cannot be avoided) appear at times to be absolutely necessary if social life is to be maintained.

A corollary of hostility is suspicion. Centuries of arbitrary rule by native and foreign predators has cultivated among the population, as a whole, a fear of revealing personal facts. The whole tenor of society is one that encourages self-esteem and personal worth and at the same time discourages the public display of possessions. While openness and friendliness are valued, suspicion is never dissipated. A popular folk tale collected by Burckhart in the nineteenth century, but still relevant today, tells of one who says in reply to an offer for something, that his sack is not big enough to hold it. The advice is precisely the opposite of that given in the popular Western maxim 'Don't look a gift horse in the mouth.' The Arab feels that a gift is just what one ought to question and the terse parable implies that an apparently selfless donor is not to be trusted.

THE BEDOUIN IN THE CONTEXT OF ARAB SOCIETY TODAY

In a sense, the Bedouin of Northern Arabia are a 'nation'. That is, groups of families possessing all the characteristics discussed earlier are united by common ancestry and by shared territorial allegiance. The basis of their identification with the 'nation' is some form of kinship affiliation and descent. The exploitation and defence of their common territorial area is effected through a universally accepted system of leadership. For centuries, this 'nation' of Bedouin tribes and their leaders have operated in the ecologically and politically shifting landscape of Northern Arabia. Only in the course of the twentieth century has their traditional flexibility and mobility been checked. Factors foreign to their universe have damaged the territorial mainstay of their society, necessitating the adoption of a new basis of identification with the 'nation' and its leaders. To understand this process

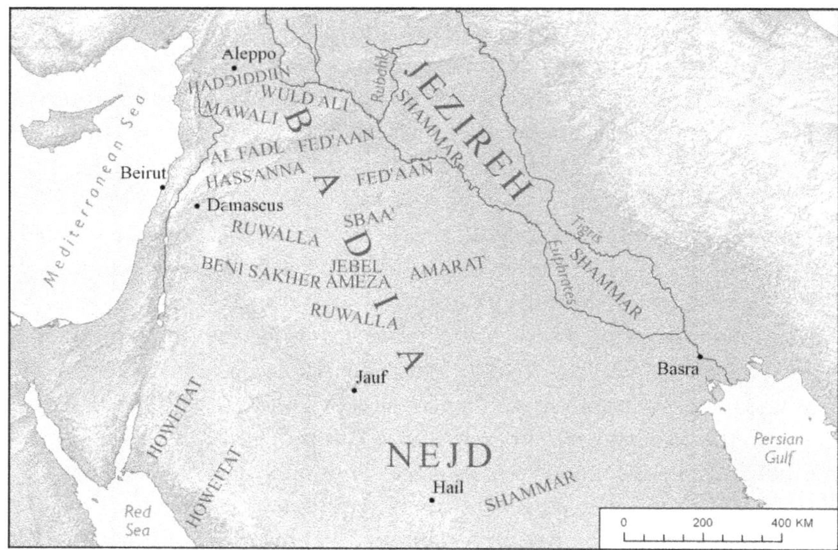

Map 4. Bedouin tribes of Northern Arabia
(approximation of major tribal grazing areas)

requires first, that the associations that underpin Bedouin tribal organization be examined. Only then is it possible to form a clear picture of the extent to which these leaders and their tribesmen have selectively adapted to the exceptional political, social, and technological developments of the region as a whole (see map 4, 'Bedouin Tribes of Northern Arabia').

Certain basic corporate interests underlie Bedouin tribal political organization. The nature of the pastoral economy, as well as its physical and social environment, traditionally requires a paramilitary organization of tribes based on a real or fictional series of overlapping kin groups. The smallest unit is generally agreed to be the *Beit* (minimal lineage). Numerous *Beits,* claiming descent from a common ancestor, then form a *fakhad* (maximal lineage). This unit, and its council of elders, is under the command of the head of the tribe. In some larger tribes, with more centralization, such as Al-Hassanna and the Al-Ruwalla, the *fakhad* head is linked to a sub-tribe (*ashiira*) leader, who comes immediately under the direction of the sheikh of the tribe (*qabila*). Thus, chains of command traditionally link the individual groups ultimately to the sheikh.

The pivotal position within the tribe is that of the sheikh. He exercises authority over the allotting of pasture and the arbitration of disputes that are brought to him. His position is usually derived from his own astute reading of the majority opinion. He generally has no power to enforce a decision and has therefore to rely on his moral authority as well as the concurrence of the community with his point of view. Although ultimate authority rests with the sheikh, it is based almost totally on his meticulous evaluation of tribal sentiment.

The tribe then is defined as a single unit through universal recognition of a sheikh and his *Beit.* Al-Fadl tribesmen, for example, universally recognize themselves as belonging to the Emir Faour (*Beit Faour*). Al-Hassanna tribesmen see themselves as associated with Sheikh Tamir (*Beit Ibn Milhem*), while Al-Ruwalla tribesmen attach themselves to Emir Mit'ib (*Beit Sha'laan*).[2]

---

2. Emir Faour-Al-Faour-Al-Fadl of Al-Fadl tribe; Emir Mit'b Al- Sha'laan of Al-Ruwalla; and Sheikh Tamir-il-Milhem of Al-Hassanna tribe. In the last two hundred years, the title of emir has been granted to a number of Bedouin sheikhs by both Ottoman and French authorities in recognition of services to the government. Al-Fadl informants universally believe, however, that their emir was one of the first tribal sheikhs to receive the title between 1199–1218. Sheikh Fadl (Al-Faour, 1968) and Oppenheim (1939) support this view.

While the *Beits* are the basic economic units of the tribe, the *fakhad*, *ashiira*, and the *qabila* are organized primarily to serve the tribal community's interests of mutual self-defence, collective pasture rights, and migrations.

With the pastoral expansion into the frontier zone of agriculture, and later into the heart of the Mediterranean coastline, an effective defence organization against non-tribal marauders became imperative. In the eighteenth and nineteenth centuries, for example, Al-Fadl and Al-Hassanna Bedouin began undertaking long spring migrations into the Bekaa Valley. This area was one of minimal security. As late as 1928, banditry was rampant in the Bekaa Valley, and villages occasionally had to pay ransom to these bandits in order to prevent bloodshed. The few male agnates of a camping unit could not successfully defend themselves against the large and often well-armed gangs of bandits. Their defence could only be guaranteed by organizing men into highly mobilized units, under the leadership of one man at the *fadhad* level. Traditionally, when a Bedouin tribe made long, interseasonal migrations through hostile territory, each *fakhad* leader organized the migrations so that all the households of the *fakhad* were ready to migrate at one time. Approximately fifteen tents moved together as a unit, while the remaining members of the *fakhad* stayed on alert. By coordinating units on the alert, and units on the move, the *fakhad* leader was thus generally able to successfully supervise the unit's interseasonal migration.

The transient nature of pasture rights shared collectively by the community also demanded an effective and highly centralized political organization. Tribal land traditionally was administered by the head of the *qabila* through a series of allocations. The physical land in use by individual households changed from year to year in relation to particular developments in the physical environment such as the annual rainfall and pasture distribution.

Rights to use tribal land also involved obligations to maintain these interests. That is, the collective property rights of the tribe required a high level of military organization at the *ashiira* or *qabila* level in order to defend or acquire highly contested pasture from other tribes. Al-Ruwalla Bedouin, the last and most powerful of the Aneza tribes to migrate from the *Nejd* into the *Badia*, exemplified this type of military organization. Throughout the nineteenth century, they conducted numerous campaigns to acquire pasture from other tribes. In 1855, they began a fifteen-year campaign to seize control of the Hauran from the Wuld Ali. In 1875, aided by the Ottoman authorities, they opened a new dispute with the Sbaa' over pasture land in the Homs-Hama area, a conflict that was not finally settled until 1931. Another example of this type of military campaign was the Fadl's prolonged fight against the Kurds, Druze, and Circassians for control of the pasture land in the Golan during the late eighteenth and early nineteenth centuries.

The gradual decline of tribal authority in the last fifty years is related to the appearance of a new element in the social environment. The arrival of the French and British mandatory powers in Northern Arabia after World War I led to the ultimate pacification of the cultivated regions after decades of anarchy.

Once French and British power had successfully instituted a form of security in cultivated regions, pacification of the tribes was attempted. After nearly a decade, the French Meharistes were able to impose peace among the Bedouin tribes along the northern segment of the *Badia*. Without infringing upon the internal administration of the tribes, the peace agreements attempted to resolve intertribal feuds and, in general, set out to protect the property rights of each tribe. For example, at the 1930 tribal conference of Palmyra, the French authorities were able finally to settle the fifty-year feud over pasture land between the Ruwalla and the Sbaa'.

Along the southern belt of the *Badia* and within the 'British Corridor', similar negotiations were taking place. The primary focus of these assemblies was, however, of a different nature. The British were mainly concerned with establishing fixed boundaries between their mandated territories and the Wahhabi state of Abdul Aziz, and thereby putting an end to the *Ikhwan* raids. The Treaty of Al-Muhammara (1922), the Uqair Conference (1922), and the Bahra and Hadda Agreements (1925) were principally interested in establishing national boundaries regulating tribal migration and emigration and thereby stabilizing their mandated territories of Palestine,Trans-Jordan, and Iraq against an aggressive Central Arabian force. Within their mandated territory, the British were more concerned with providing defensive perimeters along the fringes of the *Badia*. Their attention was directed more towards protecting their urban centres than providing any assistance to the tribes. The heart of Britain's economic and strategic interests was in the cities. The *Badia* and its tribes were seen only as a buffer zone. As long as these tribes did not threaten the urban centres, they were permitted to enter them for their seasonal purchases. Otherwise they were, as a population, superfluous to the British mandate policy.

The French in their territory, however, could not take such a benignly neutral stand. The Bedouin tribes migrating in the northern *Badia* were important elements in the rural and urban life of the mandated territory. Furthermore, they were, at times, sources of serious disturbance and unrest to themselves and to the settled population. The French mandate authorities having settled a number of intertribal feuds, took it upon themselves to go one step further and attempt to reorganize the internal affairs of the tribes for their own purposes. These measures and policies were to have profound effect upon the tribes not only in the northern *Badia* but throughout the entire Bedouin 'nation' in Northern Arabia. The activities of the French vis-a-vis the Bedouin set a pattern for similar government interference throughout the region over the following fifty years.

An attempt was made to regulate tribal pasture rights by assigning pasture areas to particular tribes and thereby reducing further the threat of intertribal war. French success in this endeavour only rendered the tribal community's own military organization increasingly obsolescent. *Ashiira* and *qabila* level campaigns became unnecessary for the protection of tribal pasture land. One example is the neutral zone established by the French Méharistes between the Haddiddiin and the Mawali tribes in 1936–37. By officially recognizing and freezing tribal boundaries the French authorities were themselves assuming the obligations to defend any tribe's rights against the incursions of others. Gradually, the basic corporate interests of the tribe were being undermined by the activities of the French mandate power.

In the late 1930s and early 1940s, the French mandate authorities introduced a new land-registration policy. Implementation of this legislation completely altered Bedouin patterns of land use, administration, and allocation. As land came to be permanently registered in the name of a sheikh or other leader, the traditional process of distributing and allocating temporary pastures changed. No longer was land distributed from the *qabila* head to the *ashiira* or *fakhad* leader to the *Beit* head and then to individual households. Rather, this chain was replaced by direct communications from the *Beit* heads to the tribal leader (the registered landowner) to determine pasture allocations. Consequently, political solidarity at the *fakhad*, *ashiira*, and *qabila* level declined, and smaller tribal segments (the *Beits*) tended to become autonomous units.

The administrative organization of the tribes continued, but only in part. Settlements of disputes and other internal affairs remained in the hands of the *fakhad* council of elders and ultimately the sheikh. However, since the tribe's solidarity was weakened by developments in the military-political realm, it frequently became difficult to impose punishments such as collective payments or *Jala* (expulsion). An inter-*Beit* homicide, for example, generally results in the expulsion of the killer for a period of seven years. By the early 1940s, cases were being recorded in which 'convicted' killers refused to accept such sentencing. The *fakhad* council no longer had the power to impose its will upon the individual. Once the guarantor of community security and defence, it was no longer an effective unit.

The sheikh's traditional authority was also threatened. Mobilization of the whole tribe in support of his decisions became difficult at times. For example, in 1923, Nuri Sha'laan of the Ruwalla decided to resist the growing Wahhabi power in Saudi Arabia. This decision was not unanimously supported by the tribe, and in 1925 Farhan-il-Meshhour left the Damascus region with 1,000 Al-Ruwalla tents to join the Wahhabi leader, Abdul Aziz. An indirect suggestion of this development was within the traditional retinue of the sheikh. A group of hired men, independent from the segments of the tribe, served as the leader's bodyguard when necessary, enforced his decisions, and sometimes disciplined recalcitrant tribal units. During this period, the number of such men traditionally at the sheikh's disposal increased. It was during this period that the Emir of Al-Fadl added an entire *Beit*, called the *Abeed*, to his personal retinue.

Thus central authority undermined the basic corporate interests of the tribal community. It also redefined and made precise the once highly elastic authority of certain tribal leaders. The leaders who had traditionally represented their communities in dealing with sedentary people, now became 'official' links between the tribe and central authorities.

To integrate the tribe into the national political system, a number of tribal sheikhs were appointed by the French mandate power as deputies to Parliament. Emir Faour, Sheikh Milhem, and Emir Sha'laan were among the twelve French appointed Bedouin deputies. These government appointments, along with their new wealth as landowners and the increased mobility offered them by motor transport, encouraged many Bedouin leaders to remove themselves from the tribe and take up residence in the major cities of Northern Arabia.

Throughout Northern Arabia, Bedouin sheikhs and emirs were creating new political roles for themselves in the post-independence nation-state.

In Jordan and Saudi Arabia, traditional tribal associations were maintained with the respective monarchs, and the Bedouin leaders held consultative voices in government decision-making. In the effort to adapt to the changed universe of the second half of the twentieth century, their traditional position within their own tribes had been modified but not radically altered. The changes in Iraq and Syria, however, were more fundamental. In Iraq, over half the members of Parliament were tribal leaders. In Syria, the former French-appointed Bedouin deputies were, in the main, returned to Parliament as elected representatives. These tribal leaders had, to an extent, incorporated themselves into the national political system. Their roles within the parliamentary system were identical. However, their position within their tribes had decisively changed. Al-Fadl, Al-Hassanna, and Al-Ruwalla leaders exemplify the types of alterations that developed in terms of authority, land, and wealth between sheikhs and tribesmen.

BASIS OF AUTHORITY

The two Emirs and the Sheikh are now elected members of Parliament. The Hassanna Sheikh is a deputy from Salamiyeh twenty miles east of Homs, while Al-Ruwala and Al-Fadl Emirs are deputies from the Damascus and from the Kuneitra districts. Their roles and duties within Parliament are identical, and subject to the rules of modern political procedures. While the Emirs and the Sheikh regard themselves as representatives of their tribesmen, parliamentary recognition is based on the size of their constituency. Officially these deputies represent a small fraction of the Syrian population. Though these leaders have assumed modern political roles in the nation-state, their basis of power is not derived from support within the general voting public, but rather from traditional positions of authority within Al-Fadl, Al- Hassanna, and Al-Ruwalla tribes.

Both the Emirs and Sheikh are members of the sheikhly *Beit* in their respective tribes (see figures 2,3, and 4).[3] Among Al-Fadl, the sheikhly *Beit* (*Beit Faour*) has been the same since the late eighteenth century, when it led the tribe in a series of successful military campaigns for pasture land. The sheikhly *Beit* of Al-Ruwalla (*Beit Sha'laan*) came to power in the early

3. 'Sheikly Beit' means the dominant *Beit*, who, having greater access to sources of wealth, provides the leadership of the tribe. Although succession need not be from father to son, it usually remains within the *Beit*.

nineteenth century, when it seized the leadership from *Beit Kaakaa'* and proceeded from one military victory to another, winning vast expanses of pasture land for the tribe. The sheikhly *Beit* of the Hassanna (*Beit Ibn Milhem*) has been unchanged since the late seventeenth century, when it led the tribe from *Nejd* into the region between Homs and Hama. Surprisingly, the defeat of the tribe in a campaign for pasture land by a Ruwalla-Sbaa' alliance in 1850 did not result in a change of sheikhly *Beit*. Although the Emirs and the Sheikh are both members of relatively well-established *Beits*, there is a wide disparity in the relationship of Emir Sha'laan to the Ruwalla, Emir Faour to the Fadl, and Sheikh Tamir to the Hassanna. This disparity results partly from discrepant bases of authority held by the Emirs' *Beits* and the Sheikh's *Beit* in their respective tribes.

The Ibn Milhem *Beit* of the Hassanna is 'one of the greatest Bedouin families' renowned for their courage and generosity. It is widely acknowledged that the *Beit Milhem* led the Hassanna from the *Nejd* into the *Badia* as the first of the Aneza tribes to move north and west during the major Bedouin expansion of the late eighteenth century. This tribe also holds a prominent position in the social order of Bedouin tribes today, since the Al-Saud family (of modern Saudi Arabia) are descendants of Al-Hassanna through the Mesalikh branch of the tribe (see figure 2).

The traditional prestige and respect accorded the Ibn Milhem family has been reinforced by a series of alliances. The most recent was a political marriage with the powerful Al-Ruwalla tribe. Sheikh Tamir-il-Milhem not only maintains the traditional position of his family within the tribe, but, as a result of his father's marriage to the sister of the present head of the Al-Ruwalla, has also strengthened his ties with other Bedouin tribes.

Today Sheikh Tamir-il-Milhem actively exercises what remains of the traditional leadership position. Since the military-political functions related to community self-defence are no longer viable, he has devoted much of his efforts to settling internal disputes. Now the owner of several motor vehicles, he has acquired the mobility to travel long distances to regulate the affairs of his tribesmen.

Disputes that cannot be settled by custom, compromise, or sanctions between *Beits* are, among Al-Hassanna, set aside until a hearing can be arranged with Sheikh Tamir presiding. These generally take place during the spring and summer migrations when Sheikh Tamir makes his rounds, visiting the *Beit* leaders at least once each season. Furthermore, the Sheikh attempts to call on or entertain the majority of the actual household heads. Once and sometimes twice in a year, he organizes a festive evening in the large white guest tent belonging to a leading landowning family in the Bekaa Valley.

Thus, Sheikh Tamir-il-Milhem's basis of authority rests not only on the pre-eminence of his *Beit* in Bedouin tradition; it also derives from his personal efforts to increase his *Beit's* authority. Furthermore, by using motor transport, in much the same manner used by American politicians, to keep contact with the 'grass roots', Sheikh Tamir-il-Milhem maintains and strengthens his position of prestige within the tribe, insuring the continued political support of his tribesmen and constituency.

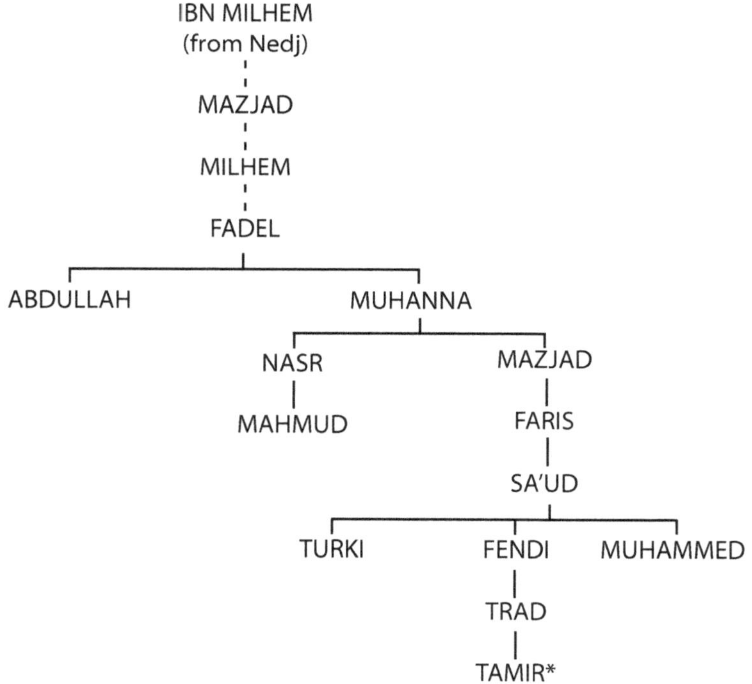

Figure 2. Descent line of Sheikh Tamir-il-Milhem

The Sha'laan *Beit* of Al-Ruwalla is without question the most famous and powerful of all the Aneza sheikhly families (Raynaud, 1922; Muller, 1931; Glubb, 1942). Their population today makes up, by some estimates, a significant percentage of all the Bedouin in Syria, Jordan, and Saudi Arabia. By 1894, Nuri Sha'laan had consolidated his control over a wide area of the *Badia* as well as the region around Damascus. The potential fighting force he commanded was the basis of the respect accorded him by other Bedouin tribes as well as the Ottoman, English, and later French forces in the region. It was during the mandate period, in fact, that the French formally acknowledged Nuri's great authority by officially giving him the title

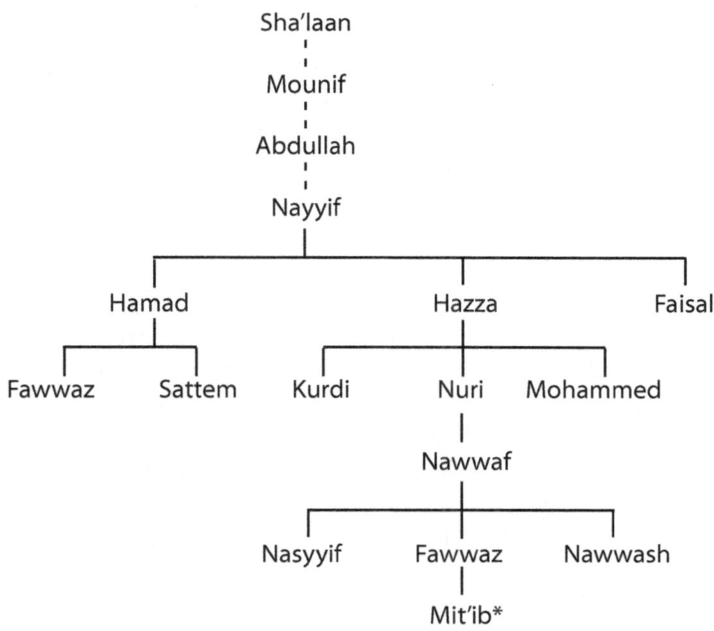

Figure 3. Descent line of Emir Mit'ib Sha'laan

of emir or prince. Numerous marriage alliances after the turn of the century with other sheikhly families of the Aneza Confederation, especially with the Al- Saud rulers of Saudi Arabia, have also served to increase the prestige of the Sha'laan family (see figure 3).

Today, Mit'ib Sha'laan actively exercises the social role established by Nuri, his great-grandfather. In one quarter of Damascus, still called the Sha'laan quarter, there is a traditional Arab house. This building, built by Nuri, is opened every evening at sunset to receive visiting tribesmen. Guests are not restricted to Al-Ruwalla tribe but include other Bedouin, and urban as well as foreign dignitaries. Emir Mit'ib in fact presides over this *majlis*, which discusses, adjudicates, or arbitrates disputes, only about six months of the year. The rest of the time he spends travelling back and forth by car to Amman and Riyadh.

Thus Emir Mit'ib's basis of authority rests primarily on the recent pre-eminence of his *Beit* in the social order of Bedouin tribes today. This prestige he continuously reinforces on his numerous trips to Riyadh to take his place at the informal tribal council of King Fahd (Al-Saud).

In contrast, the Fadl sheikhly *Beit* claims descent from Al-Abbas, the Prophet Mohammed's uncle, and the founder of the Abbasid Caliphate in Baghdad. Al-Fadl tribesmen maintain that Al-Abbas was the original ancestor of the Emir's *Beit* and the origin of the name of the tribe. Though the Al-Fadl tribe appears to be of great antiquity, the association of Al-Fadl with the present Al-Fadl sheikhly *Beit* appears to be of recent origin (see figure 4).

Al-Fadl tribesmen maintain that they were once masters of the *Badia*. Oppenheim (1939) does, in fact, assert that Al-Fadl ruled in the *Badia* during the thirteenth, fourteenth, and fifteenth centuries, but does not mention what became of Al-Fadl after the sixteenth century. The Emir Faour contends that with the rise of the Ottoman Empire, his *Beit* left the *Badia* with a few loyal tribesmen and moved into the Bekaa Valley. Although the Emir does not agree, many Al- Fadl tribesmen believe that the remaining tribesmen in the *Badia* came to be known as the Mawali tribe under the leadership of an Ottoman 'blessed' emir.

Burckhardt reports that he saw the Fadl in the Golan during the early nineteenth century (Burckhardt, 1822). Sheikh Fadl completes Burckhardt's observation by explaining that, shortly before this period, Al-Fadl tribesmen in the Bekaa Valley had split again after a feud with the Beni Khalid tribe, and the Emir moved into the Golan. Those tribesmen who remained with the Emir's *Beit* became the founders of the present tribe (Al-Faour 1968). Though some of the *Beits* recently incorporated into the tribe are clearly of non-Bedouin origin (Kurdish), the tribesmen as a whole express feelings of great pride and esteem for the Emir's sheikhly *Beit*, and, in turn, appear to be honoured by their own association with it.

Undoubtedly, the much revered Hashimite and Qurayish origin of *Beit* Faour is an asset that permits the Emir to maintain his position of authority within the tribe without continuously exercising it. Unlike Sheikh Tamir-il-Milhem, the Emir does not use motor vehicles to maintain close

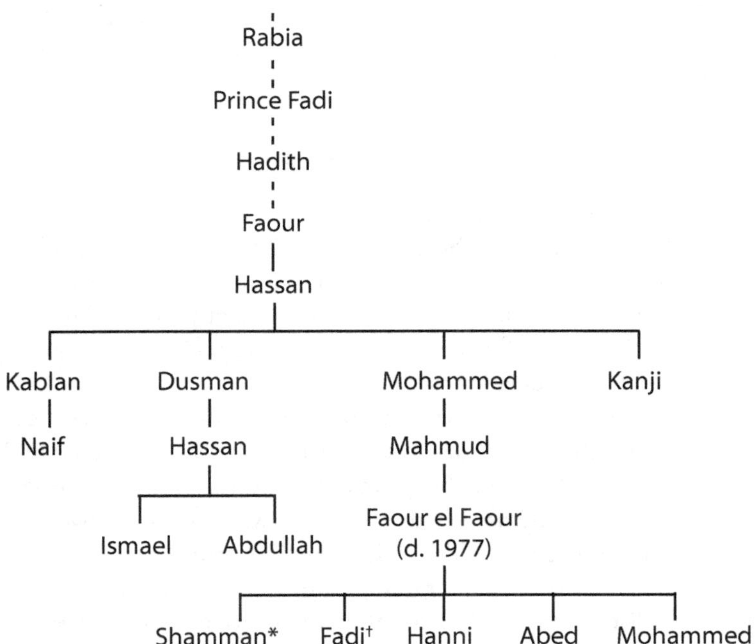

Figure 4. Descent line of Emir Faour

contact with his tribesmen. Rather, the mobility which the car offers is used by the Emir to develop and maintain his association and relations on the basis of his Qurayish ancestry. Thus he makes frequent trips to Riyadh. There, according to Sheikh Fadl and several other tribal as well as academic sources, he maintains a place on the tribal council of King Fahd along with other Aneza Bedouin leaders. The Emir generally spends the winter months in Riyadh, staying in Beirut and Damascus only during the spring and summer, when he makes frequent trips to visit the Hashimite King of Jordan.

In contrast to Sheikh Tamir, the Emirs' bases of authority rest not so much on the pre-eminence of their *Beits* within the tribe, but more so on the pre-eminence of their *Beits* throughout the system of Bedouin tribes. While Sheikh Tamir uses the car to maintain his position of authority within the tribe, the Emirs use it to reinforce their special relationship vis-a-vis the Bedouin sheikhly society.

LAND AND LEADERSHIP

The fundamentally different associations of land to leadership for the Emirs and the Sheikh contribute to the distinct relationship each has with his respective tribesmen. Current landholding systems no longer allow the leaders to exercise any authority over allocations of pasture. Furthermore, land registration and reform measures of the past few decades greatly affected the leaders' association with their tribesmen.

Among Al-Hassanna, tribal warfare for pasture land was last recorded in 1850, when they were defeated by a Ruwalla-Sbaa' alliance and lost important pasture lands in the Homs-Hama area. Thus, after 1850, the Hassanna confined themselves to areas somewhat south, between Homs and Tudmor and the Bekaa Valley. In the 1930s tribal land was registered by the French mandatory power in the name of their Sheikh. Subsequently, the Sheikh distributed land to tribesmen wishing to farm; the rest of the tribe continued to utilize the remaining pasture areas. The Sheikh settled within the area, in Salamiyeh, which became the Hassanna 'capital'. Land was still regarded as tribal property, which the Sheikh administered and distributed. According to Al-Hassanna tribesmen, their Sheikh never requested land rental payments. Instead they always made annual presentations to him. Consequently, the income the Sheikh received was in the form of voluntary donations from the tribesmen and produce from his herds and cultivated fields. This wealth permitted him to display a level of generosity and hospitality traditionally required of a tribal leader. This largesse was so renowned that Glubb (1942) was to comment that Sheikh Milhem's 'dreams of reviving the glory and splendour of past times ... together with his inheritance of his father's noted generosity, absorbs most of the revenue from his villages near Homs.'

The agrarian reforms of the late 1950s and early 1960s withdrew and redistributed landholdings registered in the name of the Sheikh among Al-Hassanna. The tribesmen continued, however, to make voluntary annual contributions to their Sheikh. Thus, despite the fact that title to land had been redefined and redistributed by the national government, land continued to hold a collective value, and traditional loyalties continued to be expressed.

For the Ruwalla, most of the nineteenth century had been a period of constant and highly successful tribal warfare. By 1894, their holdings in pasture land extended in a wide arc from Damascus southeast through the corridor that was to become part of Jordan and into what is today Saudi Arabia.

In the 1930s, the Emir Nuri set about registering agricultural land on the edge of their tribal territory in his name. In 1937, he had begun registering small plots of land in the villages of Adra, twenty-five kilometres southeast of Damascus, in his family's name, and he proceeded to replace some of his tents with stone houses. The following year he bought one-fourth of the total shares of the village. From that point on, Adra became known as the 'capital' of Al-Ruwalla and a source of private income for the Sha'laan *Beit*. In the following years, Adra became famous for the banquets held there in honour of numerous tribal as well as foreign dignitaries, amongst whom were General de Gaulle, King Saud, and the Syrian President Al-Kuwatly.

Al-Ruwalla tribesmen, however, never settled on this agricultural land, and it held no place in their relationships with their leader. The pasture lands spreading between Syria, Jordan, and Saudi Arabia remained the communal property of the tribe. Allocation and distribution of these areas continued to be conducted, as they had always been, by the tribal leaders.

Consequently, after the March 1963 revolution, when the Emir Mit'ib was forced into exile, he took refuge with his tribesmen, camping on their traditional pasture lands. Four years later, on his return to Syria, he learned that one-half of the Sha'laan agricultural property had been confiscated (over 60,000 acres) in the name of agrarian land reform. As the Sha'laan family had for a number of years been receiving a very generous subsidy from the Al-Saud family, and as agricultural land had never held a collective value among the tribesmen, the impact of the agrarian reforms on the Sha'laan and their relationship with their tribesmen was minimal.

Unlike Al-Hassanna and Al-Ruwalla, the Fadl tribal wars for pasture land were long and bitter. During the 1700s they successfully fought both the Kurds and the Turkman for supremacy in the Golan (Al-Faour, 1968). Late in the 1800s, warfare again broke out, first against the Circassians and then against the Druze. These two campaigns were concluded with official Ottoman recognition of the pasture rights and territorial boundaries of the Fadl. Not until 1887 did Al-Fadl finally enjoy the recognition of a tribal territory that included some of the interior of the Hauran and the Golan. The Ottoman government registered this tribal land in the name of the tribal leader. A large number of Al-Fadl tribesmen in the Golan then settled and began to combine farming with pastoralism (Al-Faour, 1968). Although some Al-Fadl tribesmen continued to exercise their collective rights in pasture land, cultivated land assumed a 'modern' private aspect. Rental for cultivated land began to be collected by the Emir as the absentee landowner. The Emir preferred a residence in Damascus to one in Golan. These two factors, removed residence and land rent, tended to set the Emir's *Beit* apart from the rest of the tribe. Within a few years the Emir's family became wealthy and sophisticated members of the social elite on a national level. The Emir himself married outside Bedouin tribal society, taking a wife from a well-known Damascene family.

After the Palestinian crisis of 1948, the authority of this sheikhly *Beit* was severely threatened. A major part of Al-Fadl territory fell under Syrian military rule. Central authorities, regarding the Emir as a threat to national objectives, consequently restricted his movements between Damascus and the Golan (Al-Faour, 1968).

Prior to 1949, land had been a source of political and economic power for the Emir, especially as his relationship with the tribe had become semi-feudal. After 1949, the Emir's economic strength declined greatly, as his land rental payments dwindled, and his political power was effectively suspended by his forced residence in Damascus. According to Al-Fadl tribesmen, the elders of the tribe attempted to collect the land rent themselves after 1949 and take it to Damascus to pay the Emir. But each successive year, fewer individuals were willing to pay, and finally, in 1958, payment ceased altogether.

The associations of land to leadership within Al-Hassanna, Al-Ruwalla, and Al-Fadl are thus entirely different. Among the Al-Ruwalla, access to pasture land throughout the nineteenth and twentieth centuries has never been seriously threatened, thus serving to maintain traditional leadership associations. Among Al-Hassanna, the long and relatively stable period of continual access to pasture tended to maintain traditional leadership associations. These relationships were symbolically reinforced by voluntary presentations, even during the periods of national upheaval. Among the Al- Fadl, the relatively short and heavily contested period of access to pasture did not support a traditional leadership association.

MORAL VERSUS ECONOMIC POWER

Traditionally, an emir or sheikh had greater economic resources through which he maintained his position of power. Generosity and hospitality, as measures of a leader's effectiveness, thereby, served to attract the support of tribesmen. Today Emir Faour, Emir Mit'ib, and Sheikh Milhem have each gathered the support of their tribesmen, but in different ways.

Sheikh Milhem is a relatively wealthy man with residences and investments in Salamiyeh and Homs, as well as a large herd of sheep. He maintains his household in the tradition of generous hospitality. The Hassanna, themselves, frequently remark that Sheikh Milhem's hospitality is boundless (*Karamho Mashhuur*). This hospitality even extends to periods during which his tribesmen are in the Bekaa Valley. During the summer he resides in Chtaura in the heart of the Bekaa Valley. In the course of his frequent visits by car to nearby tribesmen, he arranges numerous social gatherings, in addition to the feasts that are arranged in his honour. Thus, Sheikh Milhem, using his economic wealth and mobility, secures the continued loyalty of his tribesmen.

With Al-Ruwalla, support of the Emir is still related to the political and military empire carved out a century earlier by the Sha'laan family. But the economic wealth of the family, based on their own livestock holdings and on the generous gifts from the Saudi Arabian and now Qatari tribal leaders, has shrunk, barely allowing them to maintain their households in the tradition of generous hospitality. Nevertheless, the moral authority vested by the tribesmen in the Emir remains undiminished. The Ruwalla still look to their Emir to represent them, on an equal, if not higher, footing with the other Bedouin leaders in the modern political universe of the Middle East.

With the Al-Fadl, support of their Emir is no longer related to economic power. By the late 1950s, his landlord–tenant relationship with the tribe had come to an end when his lands were confiscated by the national government. Since a great deal of the Emir's potential had once depended on the income from land rent, he was no longer able to maintain the traditional generosity expected for one of his social position.

One incident in particular marked a turning point in the moral attitude of the Fadl towards their leader's status and role. In 1960, the Emir, having left his car where it broke down, walked to a settlement of his tribesmen. Seeing their Emir walk, while other tribal leaders had cars, alarmed them. Consequently, they set about trying to revalidate the Emir's social status, which had been threatened by his personal economic defeat. A campaign was conducted by the tribesmen to raise funds in order to purchase a new car for him. Furthermore, some *Beits* within the tribe began sending voluntary payments of sheep and goat to the Emir's household as a compensation for his material loss. In their eyes the Emir was no longer the landlord to whom the tribe had been paying rent for over eighty years. He was the leader of their community, and, therefore, he had to be maintained on an equal social level as other tribal leaders. Al-Fadl tribesmen took it upon themselves, as a moral responsibility, to see that their leader could fulfil his traditional role.

This generous response of the Fadl, the Emir maintains, brought about a change in his own behaviour as well. There was a marked increase in his contacts with the tribe and in the number of affairs he handled on their behalf. Though he did not change the pattern of his visits, more tribal elders began to approach him or be invited to visit him in Beirut. By the mid 1960s, the Beirut-based Emir was devoting most of his energy in the interest of his tribe. For example, between 1964–65, he negotiated with Lebanese authorities on behalf of his tribesmen in the Bekaa Valley. The Fadl units wanted to acquire land along the Anti-Lebanon Mountains. But, since they were not Lebanese citizens, they were technically not permitted to purchase land. The Emir assumed what he called 'moral responsibility' to aid them, and, through his intercession, the coveted land was finally acquired by these tribal noncitizens. Thus, Al-Fadl tribesmen, faced with a situation precluding the traditional association of leadership with wealth, redefined the role of emir to fit their moral system. His material generosity was no longer an issue of importance; rather his moral and symbolic position as their leader was paramount. Through the Emir, their basic corporate interest as a single community was reaffirmed.

The changes in the basic corporate interests of Al-Fadl, Al-Ruwalla, and Al-Hassanna have significantly affected traditional leadership patterns within the tribe. The organizational changes in the nation-state, particularly in internal security, land registration, and agrarian reform, have greatly diminished the political-military solidarity of the tribe. Although the tribal political organization is greatly altered, the adjustments which the Emirs and the Sheikh make to the factors of authority, land, and wealth reveal an underlying political solidarity. For the Sheikh, this solidarity is expressed in a continuation of traditional leadership attitudes and behaviour patterns. For the Emirs, this solidarity is expressed in a reaffirmation of the moral system. Yet both the Emirs and the Sheikh, in their capacities as elected deputies to Parliament, are regarded by government officials as spokesmen for an administrative region, not as representatives of their tribes. This national attitude indicates that, although Al- Fadl, Al-Ruwalla, and Al-Hassanna have successfully integrated themselves into the regional economy, a political integration is far from being achieved.

~ 4 ~

The Camel: The Traditional Way of Life of a Bedouin Household[1]

In the late eighteenth century European traveller in Northern Arabia, Volney, recorded for posterity his impressions of the Bedouin. In his diary, he wrote '*En générale, les Bedouins sont petits, maigres et hâles ... que les cheiks ... étaient toujours cinq pieds six pouces pendant que la taille générale n'est que de cinq pieds deux pouces*' [In general, the Bedouin are small, lean and tanned ... only the sheikhs are always five feet six inches tall ... while the general height is only five feet two inches] (1787:204). Although the physical stature of the Bedouin is today slightly more than the five feet two inches Volney assigns to them, they stand out as a small, dark, and lithe people.

They are further distinguished from other people, especially the adjacent agricultural population, by a particular type of clothing. The traditional male attire consists of a long dress (*thoub*) with a white or patterned head cloth (*hatta*) that is held in place by a double braided headband (*a'gaal*). The older men of the community always dress in this manner, adding a Western suit jacket to their dress for formal occasions. Among the Bedouin, as in any society, dress is a badge that identifies a man as belonging to a particular community. The cut of a Bedouin's dress, the colour and method of folding his *hatta*, and the way in which the *a'gaal* is placed on the head is generally sufficient evidence to identify his tribal affiliation.

The traditional attire of Bedouin women consists of a long, loose, dark-coloured dress (*thoub*), which generally sweeps the ground as she moves. One or two scarves (*mandiil*) cover the head, neck, and sometimes

1. During the 1960s, a unique examination of Bedouin society in Northern Arabia was undertaken by Sheikh Fadl Al-Faour, a member of the sheikhly family of the Fadl tribe. His endeavour was in partial fulfillment of an advanced degree in anthropology at the London School of Economics. Although the major thrust of his work was kinship, several chapters vividly describe the economy of the Bedouin household as it operated in the 1960s. These chapters, along with the author's own field research in the 1970s among the same Bedouin sample, provides the basic material source for the description and analysis contained in chapters 4 and 5.

the lower part of the face. Young girls prefer more colourful dresses, and their head covering generally consists of only one black scarf loosely thrown over the hair and neck. By custom, married women wear two black scarves. A simple black one covers the hair and neck, and a second gold and silver decorated cloth secures the first one in place. As with men, differences in the cut of the *thoub,* the tying of the *mandiil,* and facial tattoos identify a woman as a member of a particular tribe. Although female fashions change from year to year, alterations in, for example, the number of tucks in the bodice, or the fullness of the sleeve do not obscure the badge-like quality of the attire as a whole.

The daily life of these men and women revolves around the household. Although several households will migrate together throughout the spring and summer months, they tend to converge with households of their close kin during the long winter months. These kin-related domestic units generally set up their camp on the same site year after year. Two types of residences are commonly occupied on these sites, the *beit sha'ir* (house of hair) and the *beit hajjar* (house of stone). The *beit hajjar* is not a new innovation in

Dawn Chatty

Plate 9. Summer tent (Al-Hassanna) in the Bekaa Valley of Lebanon

Bedouin life. Its use is first recorded in the 1920s (Montagne, 1947), as one of many Bedouin adaptations that accompanied the shift in emphasis from camel raising to sheep herding.

Structurally, the *beit sha'ir* and the *beit hajjar* are alike. Both are rectangular in shape and consist of two, and occasionally three, sections. One section is the woman's domain. Food supplies and equipment, bedding, and household utensils are stored along the rim of this section, sometimes forming the divider between it and the rest of the residence. Here, women prepare all food except for bread, which is always baked outdoors or in a separate structure. The other section is almost exclusively the domain of men and visitors. The household head spends much of his time here. The focal point of this section is the coffee *mangal* (brazier). It is around this *mangal* that men will sit when a *majlis* (a meeting or sitting area) is being held. The household head is constantly roasting, boiling, or warming the bitter coffee extract that, by custom, must be served to the stream of visitors, guests, clients, and relatives. Sometimes the Bedouin home includes a third section, where sick or very young animals are cared for.

Whenever possible, food, prepared in the women's section, is served to male guests around the *mangal* on large copper or aluminium trays. Three or four men eat at a time, relinquishing their place to other men when they have eaten what they want or what custom demands of them. The women remove the trays once all the men have eaten. The remaining food (usually most of what was originally served) is then distributed to the rest of the family in the women's section. Occasionally older women, especially when well beyond childbearing age, will eat with the male guests around the *mangal.*

During the winter, families using *beit sha'ir* change from the long, light cloth tent to the black, compact, goat-hair tent. The light-coloured tent permits a good flow of air and is more suited to the hot, dry summer, whereas the compact goat-hair tent is better protection against the cold, wet winter.

Depending upon the season of the year and, more specifically, the quality of the surrounding pasture land, as few as three *beits,* and sometimes as many as fifteen, form a camping or residence unit. These units are exclusively kin based, and the lone *beit* in isolation simply doesn't occur. The term *beit* used by the Bedouin to describe the physical dwelling is also used by them to refer to the family group. In general, a *beit* comprises the agnatic unit or the three-generation family. The *beit* of Abu Mohammed

Dawn Chatty

Plate 10. Abu Ali (Al-Fadl)

is one example.[2] Abu Mohammed's *beit* consists of ten individuals: Abu Mohammed and his wife, four sons, and four daughters. Two other married sons with young families live in tents within a hundred metres' distance. The three tents form one camping unit. A slightly more complex, though quite typical, domestic unit is that of *beit* Abu Ali. This household consists of fifteen individuals: Abu Ali and his wife, his oldest son, his first wife and her three children, and his second wife and her eight children. A widowed daughter-in-law and her children live in an adjacent *beit* and is in a state of transition. At times it is considered to be part of Abu Ali's domestic unit, while at other times it is referred to as *beit* Um Faysal, the name of her recently married oldest son. Although family size in Bedouin society most frequently ranges between six and ten members, these two households are far from unusual. In fact, they provide a standard from which patterns of

2. The terms *Ab* (father) and *Um* (mother) are, in Arabic, used as forms of address. The married adult is referred to by the name of one of his or her sons (and sometimes daughters). Thus Mohammed Saalih Juma is called Abu Ali, the name of his eldest son.

Dawn Chatty

Plate 11. Woman mending tent flap in the Syrian desert (Al-Fed'aan)

daily life in traditional Bedouin households throughout Northern Arabia can be factored out.

The rhythm of a Bedouin household is very much a reflection of the personalities that run it. Abu Ali and Um Ali, the elderly couple who control *beit* Abu Ali, are a highly respected and warm pair. Um Ali, a large, talkative, and spontaneous woman in her early sixties, is the perfect foil for Abu Ali, a wiry, quiet, and thoughtful man in his early seventies. This couple, with time and experience on their side, are repositories of a wealth of tribal tradition and lore. Abu Ali is head not only of the household but also of a minimal lineage composed of all the descendants of his grandfather. This unit, *Beit* Saalih, consists of ninety individuals.

According to Abu Ali, these *Beits* could have a generation depth of five to six degrees between the founding ancestor and the living. Though Abu Ali felt his unit was unusual in that it extended only one degree beyond the three-generational family, this shallow depth was quite common.

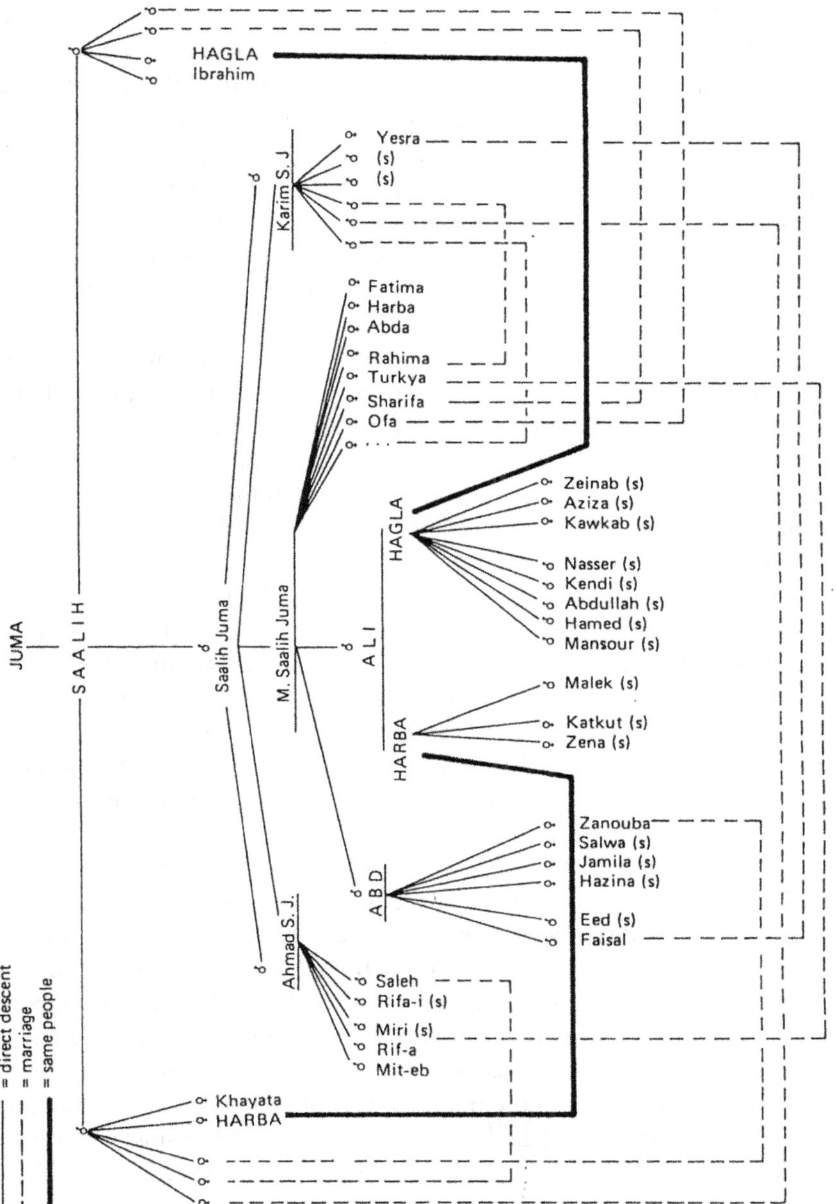

Figure 5. Genealogical tree of Beit Saalih

In fact, Musil (1938) states that these units are usually three generational only. What is important to keep in mind is that these *Beits* are the only units that appear to adhere to kinship ideology. That is, the genealogy at the level of the minimal lineage represents historical fact (see figure 5). This patrilineal descent group forms a residential community for part of, if not all, the pastoral cycle. *Beit* Saalih, for example, forms the pastoral community situated snugly along the foothills of the Anti-Lebanon Mountains for most of the year. Here, the clusters of stone houses and cloth tents are the physical and spiritual focus of the members of the lineage. This is due, in part, to the recent land ownership arrangements of the community as well as Abu Ali's year-round presence there. The members of actual camping units are always drawn from one lineage. Households whose heads are brothers, cousins, father and sons or similar combinations generally comprise a single camping or residence unit. A domestic unit can consist of from one to three residence structures, depending upon the nature of the family unit and the stage of development it has reached in the domestic cycle of growth, dispersion, and replacement.

Beyond the tangible *Beit,* Abu Ali regards the notion of the tribe as something that resembles a pyramid in shape. At the top is the *qabila* (tribe). Descending from it are several main sections called *ashiiras* (sub-tribes), each under a sheikh. These *ashiiras* are further subdivided into *fakhads* (maximal lineage). Lastly, each *fakhad* consists of a number of *Beits.* Within these *Beits,* the only named divisions are the extended families. The minimal lineages, like the *Beit* Saalih that Abu Ali presided over, are the smallest political units of the tribe.

The council of elders representing all the *Beits* of a particular *fakhad* had once been important for settling issues concerning land use, water rights, inter-*Beit* disputes, and even homicides. Decisions of such a council needed to be unanimous in order to be binding. The structural weakness of this council was quite apparent, and Abu Ali took pains to point to several case histories where the council had failed to carry out a decision. One striking example took place in 1942. An inter-*Beit* homicide occurred. The case was presented to the tribal *fakhad* council, where it was ruled by the *Beit* elders as an accidental killing. The victim's *Beit* refused to accept a settlement. Instead they left the tribe and joined the Hassanna tribe for a time, adopting a new name and a new historical genealogy.

Dawn Chatty

Plate 12. Young woman baking bread (Al-Fed'aan)

In recounting stories of the past, Abu Ali constantly referred to the *khamsa* unit, which was traditionally responsible for the defence and well-being of the minimal lineage. They formed what Abu Ali sometimes called a *diya* group, meaning it was their collective responsibility to extract vengeance for any member of their lineage who was killed, maimed, or kidnapped. In turn, any of them could be punished, killed, or expelled from the tribe in vengeance for a homicide committed by a member of their group. The story of the Fadl minimal lineage, which left the tribe in 1942 after refusing to accept a settlement of 'blood money', illustrates some of the complexities behind *diya* group action. It seems that, in 1945, this lineage expressed a willingness to accept the *diya* settlement after all and to return to the tribe. Abu Ali and other tribal elders of the *fakhad* met and decided that the *diya* should be twice the usual amount. A sum equivalent to $2,000 was collected equally from all the households in the *fakhad.* The payment was then given to the father of the victim and distributed among the members of the victim's *Beit*. This procedure, Abu Ali maintained, was taken in order to express the *fakhad* council of elders' unanimous desire that the minimal lineage in question return to the tribe. The action apparently worked, as this lineage is now again part of the Fadl tribe, and little mention is made today of the three years they spent as members of Al-Hassanna tribe.

Bride wealth, like *diya* payments, was also collected from all members of a *khamsa* unit. Marriage was, and still is, normally contracted within the minimal lineage. Basically marriage within the minimal lineage is to the closest relative permitted by the Koran (Surah 4:23). This is between a man and his father's brother's daughter. Not only is this parallel cousin marriage to the *bint amm* or *ibn amm* preferred, but in addition, the father's brother's son has a customary right to his cousin. Although the female cousin may refuse to marry her father's brother's son, she may not marry anyone else without his consent first. In Bedouin society, therefore, a device called *radwah* is frequently employed. Here a sum of money (equal to $180–220) is given to the father's brother's son to 'quiet' him, so that the cousin can marry elsewhere.

According to Abu Ali, the amount of the *radwah* varies in relation to the degree of opposition expected from the father's brother's son. In some cases, a horse, rather than a monetary gift, is felt to be most appropriate. Once obstacles to a marriage have been cleared, the question of bride wealth is faced. Normally this is set with an eye on the social distance between families. The greater the distance, the higher the bride wealth. Within the minimal lineage, bride wealth is usually one-third less than for a more distant relation. In the early 1970s, the bride wealth for a first cousin was equal to approximately $1,000, while the more normal amount came to approximately $l,500–$2,000.

This parallel cousin marriage, was, and still is, the actively favoured form of marriage among all Bedouin tribes. In some cases, its incidence reaches almost ninety per cent (Randolph, 1968; Cole, 1971). However, the term 'first cousin' in many of these marriages is often only a classificatory one. In many cases of parallel-cousin marriage, the *bint amm* or *ibn amm* are actually second or third cousins. Nevertheless, these cousin marriages are seen as reinforcing the unity and authority of the minimal lineage. Rather than creating new ties, this form of marriage consolidates old ones.

Dawn Chatty

Plate 13. Young woman dressed for a wedding (Al-Fadl)

The genealogical tree of Abu Ali's *Beit* clearly illustrates the frequency of cousin marriage (figure 5). Abu Ali has only one wife, a first cousin. They had two sons. Their oldest son, Abd, died several years earlier, leaving his wife, Harba', with six children. They also have eight daughters. All of their daughters married cousins, sons of Abu Ali's uncles or brothers.

Their surviving son, Ali, has two wives. This plural marriage is relatively unusual and, as with most such cases, is related to the issue of fertility. His first wife, Hagla, is a first cousin twice removed. After ten years of marriage and no children, he took a second wife, Harba, also a first cousin twice removed. Then, to his and everyone else's surprise, both wives began producing offspring. His children are still too young to see whether they will follow the same pattern of endogamous marriage. However, the two oldest children of his brother Abd have already contracted marriages with close paternal cousins.

Perhaps the most popular and continuously discussed subject among Bedouin men and women alike is marriage – past, present, and future. Unlike birth and death, which the individual has very little control over, marriage is a theme that the individual Bedouin feels he has a hand in. Marriages can be contracted, strained, and dissolved by the human actor. Births and deaths to the Bedouin, and perhaps to all Moslems, are beyond the manipulation of man. Marriages, on the other hand, are not created in heaven, but here on earth, and are a valid and stimulating source of discussion and activity. Marriage is a central concern of the Bedouin. This theme encompasses a tremendous breadth of subjects, revealing the intricate nature of tribal life and the fluidity with which relations are made, threatened, and broken.

This preoccupation with the one aspect of life that lies within their control is balanced by the minimal attention given to births and deaths. In fact, the birth of a child involves very little ritual. It is only several months after birth that a surviving infant is even given a name. Death, too, is treated with very little ritual. The body is normally buried within the first twenty-four hours, and forty days later, in accordance with Islamic tradition, a small ceremony of remembrance is held.

Um Ali periodically likes to 'make the rounds' visiting her married daughters, four of whom live in the community of *Beit* Saalih. Her eldest daughter lives in a *beit sha'ir* pitched less than three hundred metres from Abu Ali's tent, while her second oldest daughter lives in a *beit hajjar*, a short distance further away. Her visits have a predictable quality to them, and every other day she pays a call to one daughter or another. Usually her arrival is completely unheralded. She will enter the tent or house, move to the sitting area, and begin to make herself comfortable. By the time she has settled into the pillows and propped herself satisfactorily to one side, her daughter and perhaps one or two other women visitors will appear with a freshly prepared *nargili* (water-pipe) for her to smoke. The three or four women then generally commence a humorous and energetic narration of impending marriages, births, repudiations, and other stories.

On one occasion when Um Ali entered a daughter's home, she found that over half of the married women of the *Beit* Saalih community were crowded into the major sitting area. A crisis of major concern to everyone present was unfolding. A distant relative was travelling to their community with her preadolescent daughter. Although it did not seem to be an immediate case of repudiation, the threat of such action seemed to hang in the air. The woman under discussion was apparently on her way to ask for refuge from Abu Ali until her husband came to his senses. The problem was one where the husband had decided to marry their young daughter to an older man. The woman was opposed to her daughter being married off at such a young age, and she was going to try to get the community elders to intervene on her daughter's behalf. As few Bedouin know their actual age, girls are generally married one or two years after they reach puberty. The young girl in question was several years short of puberty, about ten years old. The woman, by seeking refuge with Abu Ali, was turning what could have remained a minor domestic quarrel into a major issue involving the future relations between two sections of the tribe.

Within an hour, the particular woman and her child were forgotten, and a more general discussion on the intricacies of arranging 'difficult' marriages was opened. Traditionally, when the normal mode of contracting a marriage was obstructed or made difficult, elopement or 'kidnapping' was attempted. This action took two forms, the first of which the women generally supported:

1. One form of elopement took place when support for planned marriage was not unanimous. In such cases, the lineage was generally aware of the plan, and an implicit consent existed. Once the elopement occurred, long discussions were held until a compromise settlement was reached. Generally the settlement was a payment of half the normal bride price.

2. The second form took place when support for the planned marriage was entirely lacking. In such cases, the act was viewed as an aggression directed at the bride's lineage. The vengeance unit was then obliged to punish the couple.

Another situation which raised a great deal of interest among the women was that of a granddaughter of Um Ali who had submitted to lineage pressure and married her first cousin. A week after the marriage, she returned to her father's household and declared that there was too much 'hate' between her and her first cousin. The marriage was dissolved, and four months later she became the wife of a more distant cousin.

When Um Ali returned to the main tent, several hours later, she found a large number of men seated at the *majlis.* These men were concerned with the same subject that had occupied the women all morning. In fact, the woman and her daughter were sitting in the women's section of the tent, while Abu Ali tried to negotiate a reasonable conclusion with the husband and his male relations. By the late afternoon, a settlement was reached, and the woman and child returned to their community with their male relatives. Had there been no settlement that day, the woman and the child would have remained under the protection of Abu Ali until such a time as another *majlis* could take place and the husband brought to reason. Obviously, just the rumour of marital difficulties brought the community together in a serious effort to mediate differences and restore a semblance of peace and harmony. It was as though any serious domestic rift would affect a large number of relations throughout the community.

This day had been highly successful, and for the next few hours, as the older boys and young women began returning from their various activities, the day's excitement was relived and retold for their benefit. Finally, by sunset, the community settled into its normal pattern. Fires were lit, suppers prepared and shared, stories told, and finally everyone slipped away to sleep.

During evenings when no particular crisis threatened to break the routine of the community, men and women would sit together and talk about the past. Since the 1920s, Al-Fadl, Al-Hassanna, and a number of other Bedouin tribes have specialized in sheep raising, relying on camels as beasts of burden. In the early 1960s, camels were still omnipresent, but, by the 1970s, they had just about completely disappeared. Sometime in the mid-1960s, the camels upon which these tribal groups relied were sold, and small half-ton trucks (mainly Toyota and Datsun) were bought in their place. Invariably these evening discussions would turn to the topic of the beast of burden, and, as quickly, a difference of opinion would emerge between men and women. Men, in general, expressed their satisfaction with the shift from camel to truck, while women, in general, regretted the shift.

For example, during a discussion with Ibrahim and his wife of the *Beit* Hajrami, Ibrahim explained that the camels had become too difficult to care for. They needed constant supervision during herding because of their tendency to move widely about, sampling shrubs and grasses. Their tendency to 'break out' and disperse during migration used to cause much damage to their personal belongings as well as considerable delay. Ibrahim also complained of the trouble that came as a result of the agricultural development of the area. As more and more orchards were cultivated, closer supervision of camels became a necessity in order to avoid crop damage. And, finally, Ibrahim complained about the feet of the camels. Their flat, padded feet had little traction on slippery surfaces, and, as more roads were being paved, camels came to be extremely hazardous. The combination of paved roads and cars, according to Ibrahim, finally turned the camel into a burden.

Women, on the other hand, were quick to defend or extol the past virtues of the camel. Ibrahim's wife for, example, would complain that in the 'old times', when they had camel and sheep, they used to have a good and easy life. 'What a difference between the large and easy life we used to have and the hard one now.' When challenged as to what was 'easy' about the old life, Ibrahim's wife explained that when they had camels, women always worked together, and in that way work was entertainment. For example, milking a camel required at least two women: one woman to hobble the animal and keep other camels away and another woman to collect the milk. She added that not only milking, but also making cheese and weaving rugs had once been pleasurable cooperative tasks for women. And, as a final point, she added that packing and unpacking camp were always entertaining in the old times, for one never knew just how many times the women, who always rode on the camels, would fall off during the journey. These grievances of Ibrahim's wife reflected a common conservative tendency associated with the desire 'to bring back the good old days'. But more than that, they indicated a very real loss. Ibrahim's wife regretted the loss of female solidarity and cooperation, which, to her, was associated with the camel.

The truck itself, as a beast of burden, was less frequently discussed by women. Their remarks were generally confined to economic spheres of activity. They expressed satisfaction with the daily pickup of milk by the dairy trucks. However, a woman had little, if any, contact with it except on the rare occasions when she was able to convince a male relative to drive her to a village or town. She took no part in the decorating, cleaning, or mechanical repair and upkeep of the vehicle, whereas she herself had once decorated the camel with woven tassels and ropes.

Men, on the other hand, were continuously occupied and concerned with the truck. During the dry season, there was not one day in which a truck parked by a *beit* was not cleaned and dusted by the men as well as small boys. Unlike other mechanical instruments (e.g., tape recorders, radios), these vehicles were constantly cared for. Scratches were covered, engines were kept in tune, dents were removed, and the body of the vehicle was always gaily decorated. Talismans and proverbs to ward off the 'evil eye' were always found somewhere on the vehicle as were tassels, photographs, and mementoes.

These units, as well as other Bedouin groups, had traded in their camels for more efficient energy machines less than a decade before. The pattern of life prior to the advent of the truck was, therefore, still a vivid memory. Sheikh Fadl reported, and Abu Ali confirmed the general impression, that, before shifting to truck transport, residence units were small, consisting of two, three, or four tents. The large, semi-permanent community near the Anti-Lebanon Mountains did not exist in the 1960s. These units had a migratory range of over two hundred kilometres through well-populated areas, and they generally set up camp in close proximity to villages, towns, and cities.

The average household generally needed to maintain certain minimums in animal resources in order to remain viable. The household of Abu Ali came extraordinarily close to meeting the standards of an ideal household. Such a domestic unit was usually three generational, consisting of a man, his wife, a married son, and his children. In time, the household head normally came to be regarded as a tribal elder. As he grew older, he gradually retired from full pastoral activity and began to spend much of the day in his tent receiving visitors, thereby assuming an advisory role in the community. Upon his death, the household came to be regarded as that of his son, who would continue the cycle. The households of other sons generally

Dawn Chatty

Plate 14. Young mother and child (Al-Hassana)

developed in the same direction so that they too eventually became heads of three-dimensional units.

In the 1960s Sheikh Fadl estimated that an average of one hundred thirty-four sheep and goats were necessary for a viable pastoral occupation. This figure falls within the range which Abu Ali and other elders themselves estimated as a minimum for household viability (i.e. 130–135 sheep and goat per household). Manpower minimums required to look after the herds included two or three young boys called *raa'i* (sheep-herder) and at least two young men called *khayaal* (horsemen) to tend the camels, particularly during the summer months, when they were rented out for transport of local agricultural harvest.

The pastoral households sampled by Sheikh Fadl in the 1960s all had a minimum of three camels to carry tents, supplies, as well as women and children during their seasonal migration. These camels were, in addition, an important source of income during the spring and summer. The camels were then 'rented' on a daily basis by farmers in the region for transporting agricultural harvest to market. The income derived from this rental was estimated by Sheikh Fadl, at approximately $900 per year per household – almost one-third of their yearly income.

During the 1960s, trucks replaced camels. The expenditure involved was calculated by placing the value of one truck at approximately the value of fifteen or sixteen camels. Several brothers or three or four households cooperated and pooled their camel wealth in order to purchase one truck. In the 1970s, the ratio of truck to household was generally one to four.

Today, camping or residence units are no longer found scattered in remote or distant areas. Generally, they are found by the side of secondary roads. Very little attention is now given to the distance between the herds and the residences. At times the household's sheep are ten to fifteen kilometres from the settlement. Given the greater distance between the herds and residences, young boys are no longer permitted to act as shepherds; older boys or hired men are preferred. Although the truck restricts camping grounds to areas that can be reached by roads, its use releases the household from the necessity of marched migrations that once were of several weeks' duration (between winter and spring pastures). With the truck, the same journey is now possible in as little as half a day.

New concepts of time and distance seem to have developed, releasing the household from many of its traditionally joint activities. For example:

1. Frequent changes of campsites in order to remain near the grazing sheep are no longer necessary. By truck, the sheep can be moved great distances in relatively short periods of time.

2. During the major winter migrations, it is no longer necessary for the whole household to migrate together. With the truck, a family and its possessions are transported in a few hours, the sheep following later.

This new perspective of time and distance has promoted a diversification of activities. After 1965, a number of households began to remain in the Bekaa Valley during the winter, hiring out their trucks and services to the neighbouring villages and towns including Zahle and Beirut. In addition, they began to utilize some of the 'state land' at the foothills of the Anti-Lebanon Mountains for cultivation.

On a more tangible scale, the truck seems to affect certain household changes. For example, food preparation, especially of cheese or butter, is no longer undertaken. Instead, cheese is bought, and more 'practical' food preparation is undertaken. Packing and unpacking of tents, which had once been undertaken every three or four weeks, has become less frequent. Before the mid-1960s, camping units moved seven or eight times during the spring and summer periods of the pastoral cycle. At the present time, a camping unit rarely moves more than twice during the same season.

With the advent of truck transport, these Bedouin were released from many of their traditional duties, as fewer migrations meant less work. The traditional method for gaining a secondary income by hiring out camels was lost to a large number of male adults. The majority of the men once involved in camel service began to work seasonally in a variety of occupations. Roughly one-fourth of them took up work in the newly developed sugar beet factories. Women were relieved from many of their traditional duties and pleasures. Feminine tasks such as camel packing or cheese making, once considered sources of enjoyment, were no longer undertaken. The burden of setting up and dismantling camps had always rested with the women. Since the number of migrations has greatly decreased, they have less work. For the married women, in particular, this has created a greater amount of free time. Rug-making, for example, was once a highly appreciated and time-consuming female handicraft. These rugs were often given as wedding presents from mother to daughter. Today the craft of rug-making

Dawn Chatty

Plate 15. Mother with young children (Al-Fadl)

is no longer practised, as the camel's hair, necessary for this craft, can no longer be obtained.

Unmarried women or young girls now collectively engage in seasonal labour in adjacent areas. This development was a direct result of the reduction in frequency of camp moves. As households became relatively stable in an area they began to form longer-lasting agreements with farmers and large landowners. At first these work agreements involved only men and older boys. By the 1970s, however, agreements were made whereby young girls were collected by trucks of landowners, taken to work in the fields, and returned to the residence units collectively. For example, *beit* Mohammed Saalih, with eight unmarried girls, has seven girls working in the fields. Thus reduced camp movements meant less work for the women, and, in turn, the younger girls were freed to earn extra incomes to support the household.

Among men, there was an increase in free time. With the superior mobility of the truck, groups of young men frequently travelled great distances (e.g., Beirut, Sidon, Homs) in just one day. Visiting was no longer

Dawn Chatty

Plate 16. Mother and daughter: the modern and the traditional (Al-Fadl)

restricted to adjacent communities, but once or twice a week included visits to distant friends and distant kinsmen.

Young boys reaching the traditional *khayaal* stage (19–20 years) are also beginning to work seasonally on farms. Part of their income is set aside for future marriage expenses. The remainder of their income is occasionally used to purchase motorcycles. To date, only a small number of young men own motorcycles. In the minimal lineage of *Beit* Saalih, just three of the fourteen unmarried young men own motorcycles. This vehicle has become an object of prestige in much the same manner that the horse traditionally was. It is being used by the *khayaal* for racing as well as games and exhibition riding at feasts or festivals. At weddings, the similarity in the social value of the truck and the motorcycle is particularly apparent.

For example, during wedding ceremonies, the bride is taken from her father's household and placed on the back of a truck with her possessions. The bride's brothers and cousins (the *khayaal*) join the head of the procession on motorcycles. Traditionally, they would have been mounted on horses and the bride would have been seated on a gaily decorated camel. The procession then moves noisily to the campsite of the groom, where the groom's brothers and cousins join in the general gaiety. For three days, races with motorcycles and cars and feasts with singing, and dancing are held. Everyone takes part – men, women, and children – except for the bride's father. Though he signs the document of marriage, he does not take part in the festivities, which 'take his daughter from him'.

Among the married women and young girls, leisure time activities are restricted to traditional patterns. Young girls have the least free time. After working from sunrise to mid-afternoon in agricultural fields, they are generally required to carry out light housekeeping tasks such as bringing water, sweeping out the tent, washing pots and utensils, or tending their younger siblings.

Older married women appear to have the most free time. Two to three hours of each day are generally spent sitting together smoking *nargili* (waterpipe), drinking sweet tea, and discussing the only subjects of mutual interest: betrothals, forthcoming marriages, imminent repudiations, and divorces. These activities, however, are restricted to the households of close agnates. As the truck has reduced the number of migrations per year, the women's opportunities to visit during migrations have been reduced.

The rhythm of the household in the 1970s has developed a deliberate and concise motion. Some daily activities are carried out alone, and others are shared (see figures 6 and 7). This pattern is now punctuated by the comings and goings of the truck.

The head of this unit is Abu Ali. In his early seventies, this basically sedentary grandfather is continuously involved in regulating and promoting the well-being of the entire unit. For example, the formal education of the children in his household is one of his major concerns. Traditionally, education was closely linked with religious duties. Children were taught to read primarily in order to perform religious duties and read the Koran. A religious man was generally hired to spend a season with the camping unit teaching the children to read and write. This traditional approach has been declining in the last twenty years. Today, between visits from other household heads and locally prominent villagers, Abu Ali devotes many of his mornings and afternoons teaching the younger boys to read and write.

The son of Abu Ali (i.e., Abu Malik) is often absent from the physical residence attending to the household's herds and other holdings. He, too, is concerned about the formal education of the children. As a young boy, during the highly disturbed Inter-War years, he had no opportunity to study either with a traditional religious leader or with his father, and is unable to read or write. Even so, the illiterate Abu Malik is prepared to sell a hundred head of sheep in order to build a schoolhouse if only a government teacher can be found to teach in the community during the spring.

Rifaa'i, the nephew of Abu Ali, is perhaps the most conspicuously absent member of the residence unit. Much of his time is spent driving a truck in numerous activities associated with herd management and commerce. Under the supervision of Abu Ali and Abu Malik, Rifaa'i is a major contributor to the economic productivity of this unit.

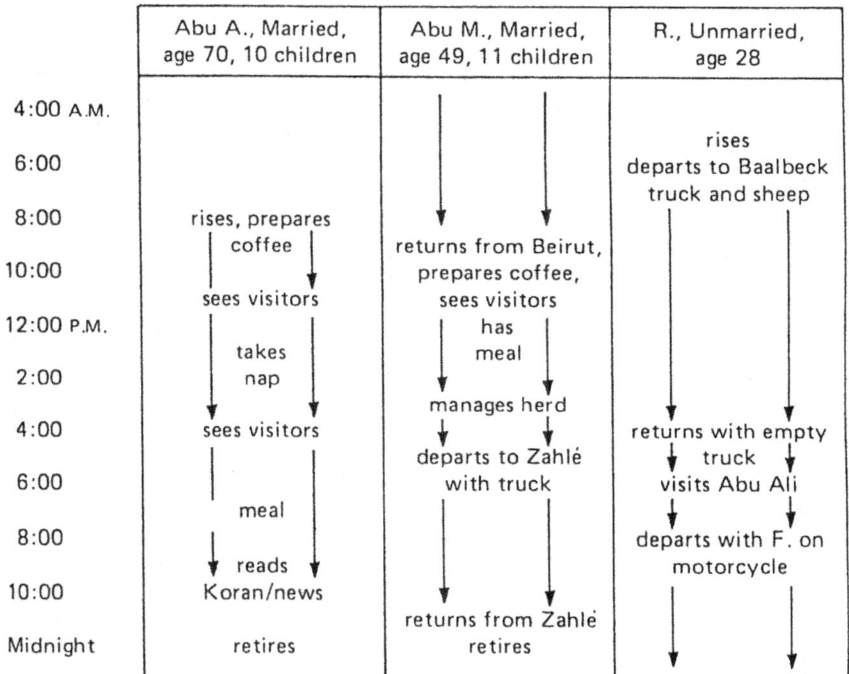

Figure 6. Daily activities of men*

* The same day applies to all six individuals of the same residence unit.

The chart has been simplified in order to illustrate the flow of activity within the residence unit

Um Ali, Abu Ali's wife, is the *Ahl-il-beit*, or mistress, of the domestic unit. Well into her sixties, she is not an active woman. However, she is continuously occupied overseeing the smooth functioning of the domestic unit. While she spends a good part of the morning smoking a waterpipe in the women's section, and receiving women visitors from other households, she also greets her husband's guests and looks after their comfort. She supervises the preparation of meals and personally carries food to Abu Ali and his guests at the *majlis*. In addition, she cares for the young children and infants during the mornings and afternoons when the mothers are generally busy with household or agricultural chores.

Um Malik, the wife of Abu Malik, is perhaps the most physically active individual within the confines of the domestic unit. Only when she

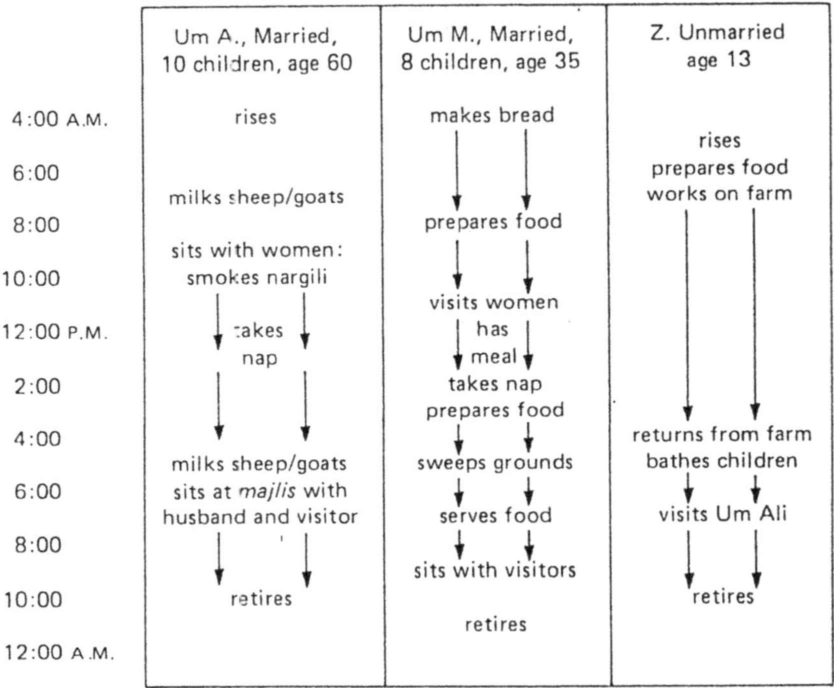

Figure 7. Daily activities of women

visits her family for a day or when she goes to market in the nearby town is she ever absent from the residence. Um Malik is the first to rise and the last to retire. Her day is devoted almost completely to household chores (e.g. bread baking, milking, food preparation, sewing, washing clothes, washing cooking utensils, washing children, sweeping, and so forth). Only when a woman visitor arrives is her activity temporarily suspended.

Zeina, the daughter of Abu Malik, is frequently absent from the residence unit. She contributes to the domestic unit primarily through her work on an adjacent farm. At the end of each afternoon, upon her return to the residence unit, she gives Um Ali her day's wages. Then she undertakes a simple chore or takes charge of the young children and infants. Though her activities within the compound are relatively light, her support of the domestic unit is significant. Zeina, herself, does not visit other households, except on the occasional evenings when she joins Um Ali on visits to married daughters in the immediate vicinity.

Dawn Chatty and Erik Shiozaki

Plate 17. Mother and child (Al-Fed'aan)

In the 1960s, before the advent of the truck, the traditional way of life of Al-Fadl and Al-Hassanna Bedouin units was relatively intact. Their pastoral cycle was, and to a large extent still is, shaped by the ecological features of the seventy five-mile-long and eight-mile-wide Bekaa Valley. Their movements in this region have always been characterized by adjustments to the dry summer and the wet winter seasons. Traditionally these Bedouin units migrate into the Bekaa steppe land at the close of the rainy winter season (April–May). Camels carrying the household baggage gradually moved south along with the herds of sheep and goat.

After the grain harvest in June, the camping units dispersed and set out to establish individual relationships with landowners in the Bekaa Valley. Each household head arranged with a landowner to graze the sheep on the stubble of harvested fields, benefitting both the farming population and the Bedouin. While the herds grazed on the stubble, they were also fertilizing the fields. This grazing pattern generally continued throughout the hot summer months. By late September or early October, the Bedouin began to return north. If the winter rains had commenced in the *Badia*, the pastoralists then moved north and east along the *qanat* system called *Sab'a Biyar*, to their traditional winter grazing land east of Homs near Tudmor (Palmyra). These traditional pastures in the *Badia* were generally in bloom during January, February and March. Once there, the camps dispersed, and a relatively idle period set in until the lambing of the flock in February or March. At the end of the winter, the pastoralists again moved south into the Bekaa Valley (see map 5).

Both Al-Fadl and Al-Hassanna conducted their major commercial activities and transactions during the summer. The slow-moving baggage camels limited their range of movement, and consequently almost all buying and selling was conducted through middlemen and brokers along their migration routes. During late winter, women began collectively to make butter from sheep's milk. This butter was generally sold to the middlemen they came in contact with as they migrated southward. During the early part of May, sheep were clipped. Wool merchants came to the Bedouin camping units and formed agreements with individual households buying the wool at a set price per animal. Once the summer harvest began, each household used its baggage camels to generate more income. A set labour rate was common, whereby one man and one camel earned the equivalent of

Dawn Chatty and Erik Shiozaki

Plate 18. Two young women and child (Al-Fed'aan)

U.S. $5 per day for transporting the agricultural harvest. Such employment generally lasted three months, with payments made in either cash or crops.

The oral accounts of household expenditures in the past were slightly higher than Sheikh Fadl's figures. But the categories were the same consisting of consumption of livestock produce, payment for agricultural products (yearly provisions of wheat, burghol, corn), occasional pasture rental fees, and expenses for tent repairs.

Income		**Expenditure**	
sale of sheep's butter		animal produce consumed	$300
sale of wool	$1430	agricultural produce	$120
camel service two camels	$900	repairs, clothes	$280
		pasture rental	$30
Total Income	**US$2330**	**Total Expenditure**	**US$730**
approximations in US Dollars			

Chart 1. Income and expenditure, household of 5–8 persons with a herd of 134 sheep, 1960s

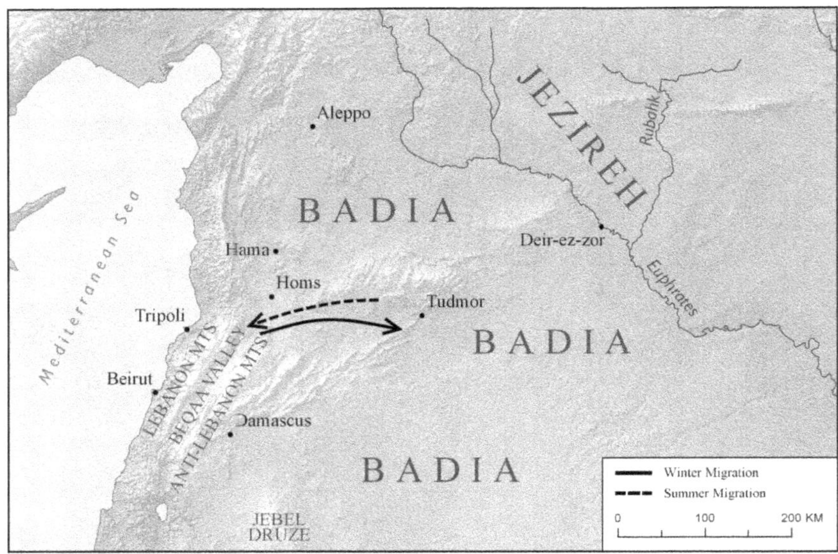

Map 5. Migration routes of Al-Hassanna and Al-Fadl tribes

The chart above is adapted from Sheikh Fadl's estimates (1968). It indicates that at least two-thirds of the net income of an average household in the 1960s remained as profit. This sum was used to meet family expenditures for feasts, marriages, funerals and to purchase sugar, coffee, cardamon, tea, kerosene, utensils, and medicine. After these expenses were met, a small savings generally remained. Traditionally, two forms of capital investment were possible: livestock or land. Aside from the risk of severe herd depletion from disease or drought, the carrying capacity of the limited pasture area in the Bekaa Valley tended to discourage substantial investment in livestock. Land was generally regarded as a more attractive investment, since there could be no loss through epidemic or negligence. In addition, land investment could yield an income for the pastoral household in the form of much needed agricultural produce.

The traditional way of life in the 1960s described by Sheikh Fadl and further detailed by the accounts of Abu Ali and others no longer exists. In the small universe of the domestic unit, the truck continually impinges on traditional patterns of activity. Its absence from the camp, and with it the absence of a large number of men and older boys for long periods of time, indicates that a totally unique sphere of activity is being conducted. The impact of the truck beyond the actual household unit, then, needs to be examined.

~ 5 ~

The Truck: The Changing Pastoral Way of Life

Dawn Chatty and Erik Shiozaki

Plate 19. Truck being packed for a move to new pasture land in the Syrian desert (Al-Fed'aan)

By the 1970s most Bedouin tribes in Northern Arabia were using motorized transport. For some, it provided more effective means of marketing their livestock. For others, this mobility allowed for an innovative diversification of pastoral activities. Throughout the region, therefore, the truck has become a significant feature in the daily routine of camel raising and sheep raising households.

Among the Hassanna, for example, the day begins early. Before sunrise, women begin stoking the fires, and mixing water, sugar, and tea in a pot to boil. Some women begin to bake the flat, paper-thin bread on copper shields, while others milk the sheep and goats. Freshly baked bread and scalding hot tea with goat's milk form the basic nourishment with which the household members begin the day. Shortly after sunrise, the herds are moved out to pasture. Then a few of the older men and the *khayaal* drive the trucks, tractors, and attached bale wagons out to nearby agricultural centres and fields. The young girls begin to assemble in the main tent, waiting for the farm truck that will collect them and take them to their work on an adjacent farm. By early morning, the remaining men and young boys begin to move about the residence unit, getting dressed, preparing coffee, or visiting one another. By mid-morning, activity focuses on the half-ton trucks used to transport sheep to market or to collect the supplies necessary for the herds. Trucks come and go, some filled with sheep, some with animal feed, others empty. A little after midday, the first of two meals is prepared by the women and served to those men and guests who are within the household at the time. If there are no visitors, no meal is prepared. By late afternoon, dairy company trucks arrive to pick up the milk the women have collected. The young girls make a noisy entrance riding in the back of the stake truck that is returning them from agricultural fields. Shortly

Dawn Chatty and Erik Shiozaki

Plate 20. Family climbing aboard a fully packed truck in the Syrian desert (Al-Fed'aan)

after them, the men and the *khayaal* begin to arrive in their assortment of motor vehicles. Just before sunset, the herds return to the residence and are milked by the women for a second time. The sick or ailing animals are given medication, generally in the form of an injection.

The day begins to wind to a close. A fire is built in front of the tent, and a large meal is prepared, consisting of bread, yoghurt, and whatever local vegetables are available. These are set by the fire, and a few eggs are pushed into the hot embers for roasting. The family, guests, relatives, and visitors gather around the fire, and the day closes with each person recounting his comings and goings or narrating adventures of the past.

The most immediate and visible effect of the truck has been in the realm of the Bedouin's annual migratory cycle. Everywhere, rapid mechanized transport has replaced the cumbersome baggage camels. In the past, Al-Fadl, for example, spent two or three months in a slow camel-transported movement northeast towards Tudmor (Palmyra) and southwest towards the Bekaa Valley. Today these migrations, including the time required to load an entire tent on a truck, take less than one day. As a result, these Bedouin enter the Bekaa Plains as early as March and remain until late November. They are no longer in balance with the seasonal pastoral cycle. In autumn, for example, the herds have no access to green pastures. Consequently most of the households depend on the *khayaal* regularly taking the trucks to town where they purchase feed concentrates – barley, bran, *tibn* (alfalfa), or *tifl* (sugar beet pulp) – for the herds. This is an attempt to offset the disequilibrium created by their prolonged residence in the Bekaa Plain.

There is, however, a limit to the amount of time the herds can remain. The sheep simply cannot tolerate the cold, wet, and windy winter in the Bekaa. Once winter sets in, the herds are moved north either into the dry shelter of the *Al-Qaa* caves, where they are given feed concentrates, or further northeast, where they graze on the pastures of the *Badia.*

Two patterns for dealing with the ecological constraints of their pastoral mode of life are popular with Al-Fadl and Al-Hassanna. Some households seed the pastures along the Anti-Lebanon Mountains with barley or vetch and then move north on trucks to the *Al-Qaa* or the *Badia* with the herds. Other households, in particular those who have purchased land but have not rented it out to tenant farmers, remain in the Bekaa Plain, and send their herds north with kinsmen or hired shepherds.

In the past the labour expenditure of a Bedouin household was primarily oriented to satisfying household needs. The marketing of occasional surpluses was always a secondary concern. It appears as though with the introduction of the truck and the concomitant reduction in migration activities, labour expenditures began to take on a market orientation. The production of household butter is a good example. In the past, women occasionally sold whatever surplus butter they had to interested buyers along their migration routes. Today few Bedouin women make butter. Most women, generally the *Ahl-il-beit* or the oldest daughter-in-law, direct their attention to the twice-daily milking of sheep and goat for commercial sales. Goat milk has a high market price and is especially valued by both urban and rural women for cooking. Bedouin households often maintain a small herd of fifteen to twenty goats, which is kept near the residence unit and is particularly valued by the women as a source of extra income.

Another example of this market orientation is the general manner in which the Bedouin have moved beyond their traditional dependence on local supplies. Today men actively search out the best market conditions for the sale of sheep or for buying feed concentrates and vitamins for their livestock. It is not at all uncommon for a household head to transport by truck three or four sheep at a time from one market to another until he finds an acceptable price.

Traditionally, the Bedouin were known to avoid main market centres and to rely on middlemen for marketing of their pastoral products. Often they found themselves drawn into particularly unhappy client relationships. Typically the urban merchants who bought wool and livestock from the Bedouin were the same families who provided the Bedouin with their yearly provisions of grain, sugar, tea, coffee, and other specialized items. Exchanges were generally on a credit basis. Over the year, a number of the Bedouin households found themselves falling into debt with these merchants. They were very much at the mercy of the middlemen, who were making large profits from the pastoral products that they bought at minimal prices. One year, for example, an Al-Hassanna household sold its wool to a merchant from Baalbeck. Rather than accept a cash payment, the family decided to have a rug made by the merchant from part of the wool. The following year, when the rug was to be delivered to them, they found themselves obliged to sell their wool to him again at a non-competitive price in order to receive the rug, which was their previous year's payment.

Dawn Chatty and Erik Shiozaki

Plate 21. Children and grandmother enjoying breakfast cup of tea and bread (Al-Fed'aan)

By the 1970s, the traditional middleman relationship had almost completely died out. Contractual agreements with large landowners and direct trade with urban businessmen were becoming common. The milk market and its tremendous growth provide a clear illustration of this development. In the late 1960s the growing accessibility of camping units gave impetus to direct trade relations between Bedouin women and local dairy companies. As the camping units became less temporary and more easily reached by road, Al-Fadl and Al- Hassanna, for example, no longer found it necessary to convert daily milk surpluses into butter in order to avoid spoilage or loss. Milk could be sold each day to the dairy companies in Zahle and Chtaura – the major suppliers for Beirut. During most of the lactation period of the ewes (between eight and nine months), these dairy companies sent their trucks to individual households to collect milk each day.

Over a five- to six-month period each year, the pastoral household receives a daily income from the sale of milk. In the 1970s the market price of milk per kilo averaged approximately U.S. $2 during the time from April to September. The daily average of milk that is actually sold by a pastoral household fluctuates greatly. This is a reflection not only of the disparity in herd size from household to household, but also of the women's own decisions to prepare certain food items such as *laban* (yoghurt) or *kishk* (laban prepared with cracked wheat) for family consumption. In Abu Ali's household, for example, daily fluctuations in the amount of milk sold involve as much as forty kilos. On some days, when special foods are being prepared by Um Ali and her daughters in-law, only twenty to twenty-five kilos of milk are sold to the dairy companies. On other days, when the women are doing no cooking or preparation of preservable items like *kishk*, sixty to sixty-five kilos of milk are sold.

Despite these variations, income from milk sales far exceeds the traditional income derived from the sale of butter. In the traditional butter transactions, it was the middleman who derived great profits after transporting the Bedouin commodity to urban centres. Now, with the removal of the middleman, as well as a rise in regional consumption demands for dairy products, pastoral households are gaining large profits from their newly established milk concessions.

Wool production, though not as steady a source of income as milk production, has also begun to provide the Bedouin with reliable profits. Here, a sudden flurry of activity takes place and, just as abruptly, ceases after

Dawn Chatty and Erik Shiozaki

Plate 22. Young mother preparing tea on kerosene stove (Al-Fed'aan)

Dawn Chatty and Erik Shiozaki

Plate 23. Young woman in 'kitchen' of tent (Al-Fed'aan)

two weeks. Sheep are clipped every year between the first and sixth day of May. Feisal, a member of Al-Hassanna, explained, 'Cutting should start on the first [of May] and be completed by the sixth; otherwise the wool falls off naturally and is lost.' During this period, there is a frenzy of activity as each household furiously works at clipping wool from its sheep.

The amount of wool that one sheep yields varies between two or three kilos. In the past this wool was sold to brokers who came to the Bedouin and bought the wool, not by weight, but by animal. In the 1960s, Sheikh Fadl estimated that the yield per sheep brought in approximately U.S. $1.60 (1968:346). Since the average market price of one kilo of wool was approximately U.S. $1, these brokers were buying from the Bedouin at 20 to 45 per cent below market prices and thereby enjoying exceptionally large profits.

After the mid-1960s, the more mobile Bedouin began to test market conditions in the area and to choose the wool brokers to whom they would sell their merchandise. The Bedouin asked current market prices per kilo of wool, meaning the realization of approximately U.S. $3 for each sheep. In 1973, unusual world market conditions forced the price of wool to rise, from U.S. $1 to $2.50 per kilo. That spring, every Bedouin household, without exception, was aware of the market situation and was determined to sell their wool to the Japanese brokers in the country, who were reportedly offering the best prices. Those frantic weeks ended in most cases with the Bedouin selling and delivering wool to Japanese concerns. In some ways, the Bedouin had become, if not an integral part of the regional economy, at least an important element in certain world markets.

The Bedouin have always maintained close relations with the major landowners and farmers in the regions where they graze their animals. With the relatively greater stability of the camping residences after the mid-1960s, individual households have begun to enter into wider and longer-termed contractual agreements with the neighbouring agriculturalists. Traditionally, these landowners hired the Bedouin and their camels to transport the agricultural harvest during the three summer months. Once the Bedouin had shifted to truck transport, they continued to undertake this seasonal service. With greater numbers of men working seasonally on the fields of large landowners, more rapport developed between the two groups. Even associations of long duration improved. A good example is the relationship between *Beit* Hajrami of Al-Hassanna and the Kez'oun family of Kab Elias. This family erects a special white tent each summer for family celebrations, entertainment, and feasts. Increasingly over the past few years, the Kez'oun family has permitted *Beit* Hajrami to use this large, six-pole tent for their own celebrations.

Rapport with individual farmers and villagers also seems to have improved in the past decade. The traditional itinerant trader, who once supplied the women in pastoral households with small personal and household items, has in large measure been replaced by the village store or gas station. Furthermore, pastoral foodstuffs, such as *laban* and *kishk,* are often exchanged with villagers for vegetables or eggs. The growing similarity in village and pastoral diet is one indicator of the gradual strengthening of the traditional relationships between pastoral households and regional sedentary households. Another example is the way in which the precious resource, water, is handled. Wells and water pumps in the region are shared. In the 1970s, it was not unusual for a villager to take water from a well on land owned by a pastoralist. Nor was it unusual for a pastoralist to use a village-owned water pump. The farmer desperately needs to irrigate his fields, and the pastoralist just as urgently needs water for his herds.

With the improvement in village-pastoral community relations, it was not surprising, then, to find young girls working seasonally with the men. The girls were generally engaged for the three summer months, picking crops such as potatoes, onions, or sugar beets. Each was paid approximately U.S. $1.50 to $3.00 per day, depending upon the type of crop being picked. An average household of five to nine persons generally had three girls as well as one or two men engaged in seasonal labour during the summer months. In some households, the income from this seasonal labour came to between U.S. $8 and U.S. $13 per day.

A comparison of the income derived from three similar economic activities among the Fadl and the Hassanna in 1963 and in 1973 illustrates the change in Bedouin economic orientation. Chart 2 shows that the average domestic unit in 1973 realized a 100 per cent increase in income over that of a decade earlier. This substantial increase can be attributed to the shift of the Bedouin from household to marketoriented production. This change is due to a wide variety of factors. The increased use of truck transport, the improved network of roads, and the resulting increased contact with agricultural as well as commercial communities in the region undoubtedly are important elements in accounting for this change.

1963			1973		
butter per year per ewe	9	$1250	milk per year per ewe	23	$3126
wool per ewe	1.6	$224	wool per ewe	5	$670
service per day two camels	10	$900	service per day truck, three girls	10	$900
Yearly Total		**US$2374**	**Yearly Total**		**US$4696**
Figures for 1962–63 derived from Fadl Al-Faour, 1968 *Figures for 1972–73 derived from field sample of 31 domestic units* *Approximations in US Dollars*					

Chart 2. Income of average household of 5–8 persons with a herd of 134 sheep, 1963 and 1973

Bedouin tribal units in the 1970s were obviously much better off than they had been a decade earlier. It was not simply a matter of seeing a number of trucks around the campsite. It was more in the profusion of material items. Almost every adult wore a watch. Whether it kept proper time or not did not matter. Every household had a number of portable radios, cassette-tape recorders, and other gadgets commonly associated with Western civilization.

The Bedouin's sudden increase in capital precipitated something of a dilemma. Given the constraints of the environment, there was a limit to the size of the herds they could raise. Only one other incentive could have pushed them to expand their productive activity: a desire to acquire land. In fact, in a sample of thirty-one households, twenty-one domestic units had recently acquired land. There seem to be three basic patterns:

1. Over half of the Bedouin households are acquiring land, which they intend to keep as pastures for their sheep. As Abu Ali explained, pastures are rapidly disappearing in the Bekaa and are being replaced by orchards. It is, therefore, imperative for them to acquire land they can use as pasture. These areas are seeded each autumn with vetch or barley to provide a good grass cover for the following year.

2. Other households are acquiring land that they intend to rent to farmers. This arrangement provides them with the agricultural products they need for their households. In addition, it serves as

a form of security against sudden herd depletion. Now that the truck has brought their traditional migratory range within easy access, some of these households are considering building stone houses on their land.

3. A few households are buying land and cultivating it themselves. Their crop production is designed to complement their pastoral production. Some fields are seeded to provide pasture for their herds, while the remaining land is planted with vegetables such as onions, potatoes, and corn. Their herds graze on the stubble of these fields after the summer harvest. Perhaps the most interesting crop they cultivate is the sugar beet. It is harvested in early October and then sold to the local factory at fixed government prices. Those herds still in the Bekaa in October then graze on the stubble of the sugar beet fields. When the herds move north towards the *Badia*, the Bedouin buy the sugar beet pulp or *tifl*

Dawn Chatty and Erik Shiozaki

Plate 24. Visitors from another tribe relaxing in guest section of an Al-Fed'aan tent

> from the factory. Truckloads of this pulp, the major winter feed, are then transported to the herds.

What had once been considered a backward economy was no longer so in the 1970s. The more these Bedouin tribal units oriented their pastoral activities towards the market demands of the area, the more their impact on the regional economy became evident. What was once described as a 'marginal' pastoral economy now needs to be viewed as an occupational specialization. As the demand for livestock and dairy products increases, their contribution holds promise of becoming larger.

A viable pastoral economy normally involves close integration of three spheres of activities: herding, husbandry, and marketing (Paine, 1971). In the past, the Bedouin were principally concerned with herding (control and nutrition of animals) and husbandry (growth of herd capital). Marketing, the formation of profits through careful circulation, was not their prime concern.

Throughout Northern Arabia, the Bedouin have traditionally focused their attention on the well-being of the herd. The capacity of the herds to grow rapidly was always balanced by the risk factors of ecology and biology, which perpetually threatened to reduce herd size. Maintaining a herd sufficiently large for household subsistence was always a major concern. Early summer of each year was the time when urban middlemen travelled out to the tribal camping units to buy whatever sheep the households were prepared to sell. Negotiations were often concluded with the establishment of a credit with the merchant. All too often, this form of exchange became one of an ever-growing indebtedness on the part of the Bedouin. Many of the wealthy families of Beirut, Amman, Damascus, Homs, and Aleppo are remembered by the tribal elders as descendants of these sheep middlemen. Although there were exceptions, these families were basically noted for their 'rapacity', which so often caught the Bedouin in a spiral of increasing debt.

With the introduction of the truck, the pastoralist-middleman relationship was completely transformed and the Bedouin assumed direct control over the distribution of sheep. Selling of the two- or three-month-old male lambs was no longer limited to exchanges with established middlemen in the markets; it now involved competitive bidding. Once these pastoralists took control of the distribution of the sheep, they began to adopt innovative forms of marketing. Though a good portion of the male lambs continued to be sold at the early summer market, increasingly large numbers began to be set aside. These lambs were subsequently fattened in agricultural areas near urban markets and sold when demand was high. The income derived from such sales was naturally much greater.

This development in livestock distribution is now widespread among the Bedouin and follows a particular pattern. The camping unit of Feisal and Gazi, two brothers of the Al- Hassanna tribe, clearly illustrates the trend. Their combined herd size, after the early summer sale of unwanted male lambs, comes to approximately four hundred sheep. Within this herd are a number of young animals that will be sold at the end of the summer, once they have been fattened. By keeping these additional lambs and fattening them, Faisal and Gazi are assuming new roles, roles once held exclusively by middlemen. Now, with the truck, Feisal and Gazi have the necessary mobility to control the distribution of their sheep, especially in the late summer and early winter, when the urban demand for livestock is particularly high.

During this season, the two brothers transport twenty to twenty-five fattened lambs to various sheep markets. There, they enter into competition with various urban brokers who are also selling sheep. The price of an eight- to nine-month old lamb in 1973 fluctuated between U.S. $20 and U.S. $30. This represents a 200 to 300 per cent increase over the price of a three- to five-month-old lamb. With only a slight increase in herding and husbandry expenditure, a tremendous increase in selling price can be realized. Feisal and Gazi, in addition to all this, keep several sheep that they take to major cities by truck just prior to the *Eid-il-Adha* (the sacrificial

Age	Weight	Price	Input expense	Return (profit)	Season
2- to 3-month lambs	20–30kg	$6.60–8.30	$1.60	$6.60	early summer
8- to 9-month lambs	40–50kg	$20–30	$6.60	$13.20–23.30	late summer
mature sheep (one year or more)	50–80kg	wide range $30+			just prior to Eid-il-Adh
Approximations in US Dollars					

Chart 3. Sheep marketing

festival at the close of the *hajj*). At this time families of pilgrims returning from the *hajj* buy adult sheep to slaughter as a thanksgiving for the safe return of their relatives.

Chart 3 attempts to illustrate the large profit gains that come from delayed selling of sheep (drawn from 1973 figures of the household of Feisal and Gazi).

A second example of the new pattern of livestock distribution is the household of Mahmoud Al-Kaasim of the Al- Hassanna. This unit is made up of a husband, wife, two daughters, who work seasonally on adjacent farms; and three sons, who tend the family herds. After the early summer sale of unwanted lambs, Mahmoud's herd comes to approximately one hundred and sixty sheep, including a number of lambs he intends to sell at the end of the summer, after they have been fattened.

From previous years' profits, Mahmoud saved sufficient income to buy seven donums of land, on which he grows barley and vetch to feed his herds. Mahmoud has also erected a special tent in which he keeps the young lambs that he sets aside in early summer for fattening and sale when market prices are good. He also keeps several mature sheep, which he is preparing to sell on special feast occasions.

Like Feisal and Gazi, Mahmoud transports the fattened lambs in the late summer or early winter to various sheep markets in the region. There he enters into competition with others who are also selling sheep. By taking an active control over the distribution of his herd, Mahmoud expects to realize a 200 to 300 per cent increase in the price of lambs.

An even more prominent example of this entrepreneurial pattern in sheep distribution is the case of Guraib Jum'a of the Fadl. Guraib, a man close to forty years old, is unmarried. His household consists of himself, his mother, and a young brother in his late teens. This household is unusually wealthy in comparison to other Al-Fadl and Al-Hassanna households, as it owns approximately four hundred head of sheep after the late spring-early summer sale of 'unwanted lambs'.

Guraib, his brother, and two hired shepherds tend the herd. In 1971 Guraib needed only one hired shepherd to look after the livestock, as he had sold most of his lambs in the spring. He maintains, however, that the profits he gained in 1971 from the sale of the few lambs he had set aside for fattening and selling in early winter convinced him to undertake the same venture on a larger scale in subsequent years.

The large profit Guraib expects to gain will, he says, be invested in the herd for special feed concentrates, wages for two or more hired shepherds, and the purchase of a small car to supplement the half-ton truck he already owns. It appears as though Guraib, with the necessary mobility to control the distribution of his herd, is methodically transforming his traditional animal husbandry activities into a 'modern ranching' enterprise.

The substantial profits many Bedouin tribal units have begun to realize from marketing and distributive activities are, in part, being reinvested in the traditional holdings of land and livestock. Individual herds are growing slightly, given the limits of pasture carrying capacity and manpower. Land holdings, though scattered, are rapidly increasing. This increase in wealth, however, has not led to sedentarization and discontinuance of pastoral pursuits. Fredrik Barth, one of the pioneers in the study of nomads, hypothesizes that sedentarization and discontinuance of pastoral pursuits take place under two conditions: 'upward mobility' and 'downward mobility' (1964, 1962).

'Upward Mobility' occurs when prosperous pastoral households reinvest their capital savings. Since only a small part of their capital can be reinvested in livestock, the major portion has to be invested in land. As land holdings increase, these households come to be assimilated into the elite landowning sedentary society.

'Downward Mobility' occurs when pastoral households are progressively depleted of their herds through accident, negligence, or debt. As the herd size becomes smaller, the household is forced to work increasingly in sedentary occupations. A stage is finally reached wherein their poverty results in complete assimilation into the landless peasantry.

These patterns of sedentarization by 'upward' and 'downward' mobility put forward by Barth, do not appear to be widespread among Bedouin tribes such as Al-Fadl and Al-Hassanna. On the contrary, though a wide variety of residence patterns are found today, pastoral pursuits of herding, husbandry, and marketing continue to receive careful attention and management. In other words, though the Bedouin are expanding their economic pursuits, they are neither losing contact with their pastoral community nor leaving their pastoral pursuits in order to supervise and control property holdings.

The introduction of a new element, the truck, is a possible explanation of the inapplicability of the patterns of sedentarization described by Barth. Among Al-Fadl and Al- Hassanna, for example, it seems that 'upward' and 'downward' mobility do not necessarily imply eventual sedentarization in the status of 'propertyless villager' or 'sedentary landlord'.

Once Bedouin tribes such as the Fadl and the Hassanna were able to control the marketing of sheep effectively, some individuals within these communities began to develop the potential of truck transportation even further. These individuals assumed an entrepreneurial role within the regional market. They began buying lambs at the early-summer sheep market, distributing them among their herds or those of their kinsmen and reselling the fattened animals at a time when the demand for meat was especially high.

The domestic unit of *beit* Abu Ali is a good example of this type of activity. This household holds capital in land and livestock. In 1973, while Abu Ali attended to the duties of an elder, his son, Ali, acquired and worked ten donums of land growing, among other crops, sugar beets. This crop, he sold at a fixed price to a local factory. His livestock holdings were relatively small, consisting of about sixty sheep and fourteen household goats. In early summer he bought one hundred lambs at the sheep market with the money he had earned by selling his agricultural harvest.

In late summer he began a systematic marketing of these fattened sheep. On some days he transported a few sheep to a nearby town for sale, and on others he drove to more distant points with the sheep he wanted to sell. In each case, the marketing of these sheep meant an income of 200 to 300 per cent over his original investment. By the time winter had set in, he had marketed all the original one hundred lambs throughout the region.

By investing the income he earned from a government sponsored crop into an innovative 'ranching' or husbandry activity, Ali was not following traditional capital investment patterns. His progressive increase in herd capital, or to use Barth's term 'upward mobility', has not led to his assimilation into the sedentary community. On the contrary, his entrepreneurial investments are being used to perpetuate his pastoral activities, not his real-estate holdings. His concern is to manage and develop his pastoral activities rather than to develop land or property interests.

'Downward mobility', or the progressive loss of herd capital, has not signalled the end of pastoral activities either. Sheikh Hamdaan of Al-Fadl is a good example of an individual who, despite greatly depleted herds, is making an effort to keep to the pastoral way of life. This man has four sons, two of whom work seasonally in sugar beet factories. In the summer of 1973, he bought forty lambs from the sheep market, which his younger sons herded throughout the summer. By early winter, most of the fattened lambs had been taken by truck and sold at relatively high prices. The large income from these sales permitted Sheikh Hamdaan to supply his household with winter provisions without incurring a debt. Next year, he says, he may be able to buy a larger number of lambs in the early summer, and perhaps increase his herd capital. By effective utilization of the truck, households whose herds have been greatly depleted no longer inevitably pass from the pastoral to the sedentary agricultural society. Some households, such as that of Sheikh Hamdaan, are able to integrate their economic activities successfully into the regional economy by maintaining a diversity of pastoral and agricultural pursuits. The incomes from seasonal labour serve as the basis upon which careful sheep husbandry and distribution is undertaken. The higher profit from this last activity successfully curbs the traditional trend of sedentarization, which Barth describes as 'increased dependence on sources within a village, and eventual integration into the sedentary community' (1964:109).

Among the Bedouin, increased mobility has permitted a diversification of pastoral activities closely attuned to regional market demands. Some of these activities have moved beyond strictly pastoral pursuits, though they are logical extensions of the traditional economy. Over the past fifteen years, for example, the Fadl have achieved regional recognition for their contribution to the *maslakh* (slaughterhouse) district of Beirut. The events that led to the development of their quasi-monopoly of mutton distribution in Beirut are well known. In the mid-1960s, three Al-Fadl households sold all their livestock and moved to Beirut. They settled in the *maslakh* district of the city and began a series of activities that involved buying, slaughtering, and distributing mutton to butchers and supermarkets throughout the city. These households are uncommonly successful, perhaps due in part to the management and circulation of resources through a kinship network. Sheep are procured by kinsmen either from their own herds or from nearby sheep markets. The actual distributors are individual members of Al-Fadl tribe in the Bekaa Valley. They serve as links between the market demands in the city and supplies in the rural areas. In 1973, estimates from butchers and market owners in Beirut placed Al-Fadl contribution to the meat market at one-fourth to one-third of the total supply.

One example of a sheep distributor is Saalih, a man in his forties. He owns land in the Bekaa, one part of which is used for pasture, and the other rented to farmers. His herds number about three hundred head and are looked after by hired shepherds. In addition, he and his three brothers are building a stone house on a small plot of land along the Anti- Lebanon Mountains. By effectively utilizing the truck, he has developed a profitable economic association with the regional livestock market. Demands in Beirut, channelled through Al- Fadl kin in the *maslakh*, are rapidly supplied by him in the Bekaa. His commercial activities also involve a more classic 'middleman' role. When sheep prices are high in one market and low in another, he buys sheep from the lower-priced market and transports and sells the sheep at the higher-priced market. These commercial and transportation activities are not carried out alone, but require the assistance of his brothers and cousins, the male agnates of the *Beit.* The nature of these commercial and transport enterprises brings the male agnates of a *Beit* together in time-consuming, cooperative activities affecting not only economic, but also social and political aspects of their total organization.

Saalih is the 'coordinator' of this commerical and transport enterprise (see Dalton, 1969). His greater economic strength does not interfere with the traditional leadership of Abu Ali, the *Beit* elder, but reinforces it. Saalih is more interested in giving support and distributing profits within the *Beit* since his activities require their backing and assistance. For example, when Saalih receives information concerning discrepancies in buying and selling prices at various markets, he goes to the *majlis* of the head of the *Beit.* There, he, his brothers, and his cousins discuss with Abu Ali the possibilities before them, and a group decision is made as to the number of sheep to be bought. Each of these male agnates participates in the purchasing and eventual sharing of profit.

The actual commercial transactions of this enterprise are carried out by two of the male agnates, usually Saalih and a brother or cousin. In October 1973, for example, when a discrepancy of approximately U.S. $3 was found between two sheep *suqs* (markets), Saalih and several male agnates of the *Beit* bought, transported, and resold eighteen sheep in one day. The profit of well over U.S. $35 for the day's work was then divided among the participating male agnates. This innovative activity was, of course, beneficial to the regional economy as well, since it tended to alleviate some of the discrepancies in market distribution of livestock.

Saalih and his male relatives, as well as structurally similar groups, have not limited their 'middleman' activities to short-term and long-term buying and selling of sheep. When, for example, there is a sufficiently high demand for any commodity in Beirut, Saalih and his associates engage in relatively more time-consuming and distant undertakings in order to procure the commodity and deliver it for distribution in Beirut. Such interstate activity, involving higher risks but greater profits, follows set and established routes to the north and southwest into Syria and Jordan.

In the late summer of 1973, for example, very few watermelons reached the Beirut market. Saalih and his cousins arranged to send two trucks across the Anti-Lebanon Mountains to Zebdani, in Syria, in order to collect a shipment of watermelons arriving from Jordan. This particular endeavour required four men and over fourteen hours for completion. Once the shipment was delivered to Beirut, the men returned to the *majlis* of Abu Ali. The profit from this commercial transaction was distributed equally among the participants. The chart below illustrates the range of commercial and transport activities undertaken by Saalih and the male agnates of his *Beit.*

	Distribution of sheep	**Circulation of sheep**	**Distribution of nonpastoral commodity**
Time	9:00 p.m. to 10:00 a.m.	3:00 p.m. to 10:00 p.m.	8:00 p.m. to 10:00 a.m.
Persons	Saalih and a brother	Saalih and a cousin	Saalih, two brothers and a cousin
Activity	sale of eight sheep from herd to market in Marj'ayoun	buying of eight sheep from Baalbek for resale in Nabatea (twice)	two trucks transport commodity froim Zebdani
Approximations in US Dollars			

Chart 4. One week in late summer (1973) selected in order to illustrate the range of commercial activities in which the truck is used

The new social roles necessary to carry out these activities are compatible with the traditional economic roles within the *Beit.* There is no reallocation of resources, only a fuller and more profitable use of them. The organization of male agnates to conduct new commercial activities does not conflict with traditional duties. In fact, there is a striking similarity in the patterns of recruitment and organization of this group, with the recruitment and organization of the now largely obsolete *ghazu* group. The latter traditionally conducted raids for livestock against other tribal units and was composed of a small number of the male agnates in a *Beit.* Its leader, the *'aqiid*, was removed from political leadership. He was chosen for personal qualities necessary for the group's successful undertakings (Musil, 1928). The *ghazu* and its leader gradually ceased to function during the Inter-War Mandate. By the mid-1950s, raids conducted by the *ghazu* group were effectively controlled if not eliminated. Men who had once been recruited into the *ghazu* groups are now recruited into units undertaking innovative commercial activities. In addition, the traditional role of *'aqiid* in the *ghazu* group is now filled by the 'coordinator' of the units undertaking the innovative, and often interstate, commercial activities.

Unofficial government policy of benign neglect has permitted the Bedouin to utilize fully their physical and technical environment. With improved roads, the Bedouin have been able to manage and expand their pastoral production effectively. Consequently, they are now expanding husbandry practices so as to include a larger number of sheep for fattening and eventual marketing throughout the year. This diversification, in which the truck is a key factor, has resulted in the integration of the pastoral specialization into the regional economy.

The economic development of the Bedouin corresponds remarkably with the urgent recommendations of the Food and Agriculture Organization to national governments in Northern Arabia. The F.A.O. views the development of the livestock sector as a crucial issue if consumption demands are to be met in the future. It recommends that a stratified pattern of sheep production be encouraged. This calls for sheep rearing to be concentrated in the *Badia* or steppe land, and sheep fattening to be undertaken close to urban markets (F.A.O., 1972). This stratification naturally implies a close integration of pastoralism with agriculture.

By focusing on two particular tribes, an attempt has been made to describe and analyze the changing way of life of the Bedouin of Northern Arabia. At the same time, an effort has been made to examine the impact which the shift from camel transport to truck transport has had on their life mode. On the whole, the basic value system of the Bedouin was reinforced by the changes generated in the shift from camel to truck. As neither the camel nor the truck was the major focus of activity itself, basic values were not altered. The truck did, in fact, support their traditional value system. The basic corporate unity of the tribes expressed through their recognition of an emir or sheikh increased. Kinship values, expressed in new cooperative activities, deepened. Economic activities related to animal husbandry also increased. Thus, basic political, kinship, and economic values were reaffirmed. If values are responsible for the direction of social behaviour, then a change in values means a change in social behaviour. The fact that many young boys and *khayaal* still tend their fathers' herds rather than work as labourers elsewhere for most of the year indicates that the basic prestige and value system of the Bedouin remains unaltered.

Literature on modernization is full of authoritative statements that hold that structural change in the economy and society of traditional communities is a prerequisite for development. The Bedouin, however, are modernizing without fundamentally restructuring their society. The recent introduction of the truck has served to emphasize the unique nature of the pastoral adaptation. Contrary to widespread beliefs, pastoralism is not a backward entity or an anachronism that stands in the way of national progress. Rather it is an integral part of the general culture prevailing in Northern Arabia. It is one of several sectors tied in relations of interdependence and reciprocity with other parts of the cultural picture. The resistance or reluctance to change so often ascribed to pastoralists is less a matter of resistance *per se* than a matter of self-interest. What is of value for one community or urban centre is not necessarily beneficial to another. Pastoralists have been, naturally, resistant to government efforts and programs designed to end their way of life altogether.

When Bedouin are not accused of resisting change, they are branded as degenerating. Any change on their part is viewed as a sign of decadence and a step in the direction of permanent settlement. The changes among the Bedouin over the last one hundred years are, in essence, responses to changes in their physical and social environment. Their loss of domination over agricultural communities necessitated the development of closer economic relations with sedentary communities. Such an adaptation ought not to be regarded as evidence of a system in decline. Rather it needs to be viewed as a system adapting to new factors – a potentially modernizing form of pastoralism.

~ 6 ~

Conclusion: The Bedouin in the Modern World

Throughout North Arabia, sheep, the traditional herding animal of the 'common' Bedouin tribes has replaced camels as the herding animal of the 'noble' tribes. This general pattern, motivated by underlying economic considerations, is widespread in Syria, Saudi Arabia (Bonnenfant, 1977), Iraq, and Jordan (Abu Jaber, 1978). In Saudi Arabia, Iraq, and Syria, the 'noble' Shammar and Aneza tribal confederations have all shifted to sheep raising. In Jordan, the 'noble' Beni Sakher and Howeitat have also taken up modern sheep raising. The richer 'noble' tribes now herd sheep deep into the *Badia* with the help of modern technological equipment such as the half-ton truck and water camion. These tools permit the Bedouin greater range and mobility in terms of grazing access, campsites, and water resources. The 'common' Bedouin tribes continue to herd sheep mainly along the borders of cultivation, the frontier areas, which can be marginally exploited for either agriculture or pastoralism.

This modernizing way of life in the Northern Arabian Plateau seems to follow two basic patterns today:

1. Tribal units in the *Badia* who traditionally raised camels, have begun increasingly to raise sheep instead. The rapid decline in the camel market, as well as the increased range of movement permitted by the truck, in large measure, accounts for this shift. These former camel raising tribal units can now raise sheep in larger numbers for increased marketing in areas never before accessible to them. The truck is now used to bring water to the herds, as well as to transport the herds to distant pastures or markets.

2. Tribal units on the fringes of cultivated land or in marginal areas of cultivated ranges have begun to emphasize particular aspects of their livestock production, especially milk production. The truck here is used to bring feed to the herds as well as to transport the herds to distant markets.

Dawn Chatty and Erik Shiozaki

Plate 25. Author with young mother and children (Al-Fed'aan)

Over the past fifteen years, among Bedouin tribes in Syria, Iraq, Saudi Arabia, and Jordan, the Datsun and Toyota half-ton trucks have become a common sight. These vehicles serve basically to transport households and livestock from one camp to another and to carry water to the herds when deep in the *Badia.* Furthermore, the truck greatly facilitates the commercialization of sheep raising. It carries feed supplements to the herds and returns the fattened sheep to markets for sale. The truck also provides for easy and continuous relations between the village and tribal camp, permitting many Bedouin families to undertake a secondary work activity in urban or village centres near their tribal grazing lands.

The settlement of Marhoum, seventy kilometres from the town of Raqqa, along the Euphrates River, is one such example. This settlement around the wells of *Aswad-il-Tasha'* belongs to the Fed'aan tribe. It is made up of approximately one hundred households. In winter and spring, however, it has the appearance of a deserted settlement. In summer and autumn, most of the households return to the settlement from the interior of the

Badia and set up their tents within a five-kilometre radius of the few stone structures that surround the wells.

Their link with Raqqa and the nearby town of Tabqa is strong. They rely on these centres for medical facilities, general supplies, and social services. Their children attend schools there, and the older boys, especially when they are not the oldest sons of households, frequently have jobs as labourers, drivers, and mechanics in these towns. One-half of the households are members of the official sheep union located in Raqqa. Many of these households have over a thousand head of sheep. Water is brought from the Euphrates River at the town of Tabqa by tankers during the dry summer season to augment existing sources.

A number of these Bedouin families maintain permanent stone houses in town as well. Abu Farhan, for example, has a permanent home in Raqqa. He has four sons, of whom only the oldest is involved in sheep husbandry. The three younger sons are all students, two having reached university level in law and engineering. Abu Farhan spends only four or five months of each year in Raqqa. For most of the year, he and his oldest son, who undoubtedly will take over the family sheep business, are in the *Badia* with the herds or on their large sheep-fattening lot thirty kilometres north of the town. The women and children of the household remain in Raqqa throughout the year, joining Abu Farhan and his son only during school holidays. This family has successfully developed sheep husbandry into a highly profitable modern business. Besides the permanent home in town and the sheep-fattening station, the family runs a cheese factory. The household members who supervise the smooth running of these diverse operations keep in constant communication with one another by truck and by telephone.

The very rapidity with which the truck is replacing camel transport among the Bedouin is, however, becoming a threat to the long-term viability of this way of life. In the past, range usufruct depended upon two factors. First, two or three weeks were required to move from one pasture area to another. Today, with the truck, one day may suffice. This mobility has in the past few years led to increased overgrazing and growing desiccation of the range lands. Second, the seizure of tribal territory – and its transformation into state land – has removed the tribal leaders from the protective and regulative role they once fulfilled in the pastoral community. In addition, the expeditious transport of sheep and wood from the interior range land for sale in market centres is rapidly magnifying the menace of overgrazing of the desert steppe. And, finally, as the demand for meat and dairy products increases in towns and villages, larger and larger flocks of sheep are being raised by the Bedouin along these mechanized lines to meet market demands. Given all these factors, perhaps the truck should be regarded as a mixed blessing for the Bedouin.

Fortunately some government administrators and development experts in North Arabia have begun to recognize the ambiguous advantage of the truck. Following the failure of most of the earlier attempts to settle the pastoralists, the governments of Iraq, Syria, Jordan, and Saudi Arabia have begun to reassess their priorities. Over the last decade, these governments have cautiously initiated programs aimed at more effectively integrating their pastoral communities into the regional economy. They have also drawn up plans to optimize the output of the semi-arid steppe in the only manner it can be used – for grazing.

Over the years the ecologically fragile semi-arid steppe land has slowly succumbed to the pressure of overgrazing, cutting of woody plants for firewood, and ploughing of marginal areas for precarious grain production. Vast areas that had once been good grazing land have become barren and are now considered man-made deserts. With the advent of the truck, as well as the transformation of tribal territories into state land, the pace of erosion has accelerated and extensive areas of range land are lost annually. As animal husbandry is an important part of the agricultural sector of the regional economy (in Syria alone, it accounts for 35 per cent of the nation's agricultural output), the rapid deterioration of the range land is coming to be recognized as an urgent problem.

In 1959, at the end of a series of drought years in which over two million sheep died, Syria endeavoured to develop its range and sheep resources by setting up range research stations. This was followed several years later by a World Food Program to develop 'Nomadic Sheep Husbandry'. The major shortcoming of this project, however, was that the human population concerned was completely overlooked. That is, while pastures were demarcated into special grazing districts, no attempt was made to organize the Bedouin and their sheep into groups that could facilitate the introduction of control measures.

During this period, an F.A.O. official, Dr. Omar Draz, began publishing reports that indicated that the rapid deterioration of the range land was due mostly to factors beyond the control of the Bedouin, the people who were always held to blame. The lack of property rights was the real cause of overgrazing and the misuse of resources. Traditional rights of usufruct claimed by most tribes on certain range sites had been revoked by the government shortly after independence. This had opened the gate for a destructive system of free, uncontrolled grazing. With the enactment of the Agrarian Land Reforms, whatever control the landowning tribal sheikhs still held evaporated as their large estates were confiscated.

Along with a handful of converts, Dr. Draz launched a campaign to convince the agencies concerned with range land deterioration of the importance of studying the human factor. Unless development programs were in harmony with the customs and ways of life of the pastoral population, then the whole range land development scheme would fail, just as the settlement projects of a decade earlier had failed. Bedouin as well as government cooperation was required in order to solve the problem. A study of the traditional Bedouin system of range management (*hema*) opened the way to a solution. In early Islamic times, *hema* was a system of setting up fodder reserves for the preservation of the 'strength of the Islamic community'. Dr. Draz suggested that if the former grazing rights of the Bedouin tribes were restored to them, a marked regeneration of the range land would take place. The prevailing destructive attitude towards the range as a no man's land open for free grazing would be transformed into a constructive one based on controlled grazing.

Range land was donated by the government to form *hema* centres. Between 1969 and 1973, eight *hema* cooperatives were established. Their success paved the way for the extension of this system – by 1976, over one and a half million hectares of steppe land and a total of twenty-two cooperatives. Sheep-fattening cooperatives were also set up on an experimental basis to work as buffers against anticipated losses in dry years, to control the rapid increase in the sheep population, and to reduce grazing pressure on the steppe. Indirectly, the cooperatives were expected to stimulate fodder crop production. In 1968, the first fattening cooperative was started with sixty-eight members. By 1976, there were a total of forty-eight sheep fattening stations with 3,178 members who operated the dry lot fattening yards.

Expansion of ploughing and grain production in the heart of the Syrian steppe region during the last fifty years has also served to destroy the vegetation of the most productive part of this large region. Introduction of mechanical equipment and increased need for grain has accelerated this progress. In 1973, the Syrian Parliament endorsed a legislative decree prohibiting ploughing and cultivation of range lands within the steppe region. In 1976, more than 150,000 tons of wheat and barley were confiscated through enforcement of this law.

The revival of the *hema* system and its successful introduction in the form of cooperatives acceptable to both the Bedouin and government officials has made it possible to stimulate a series of constructive activities. With the organization of the Bedouin in range and sheep cooperatives, it has been possible to develop a few services such as credit facilities, veterinary programs and schools. Plans are now being studied to develop a separate women's service to promote the production and distribution of cheese.

By the late 1970s *hema* participation was primarily Bedouin, and each station was run with very little interference from the government. Membership in each cooperative was basically along tribal lines. The internal hierarchy of each unit followed traditional concepts of leadership. These cooperatives were spread over most of the *Badia* in Syria and fell in areas that were once the traditional pastures of the more powerful 'noble' Bedouin tribes (see map 6).

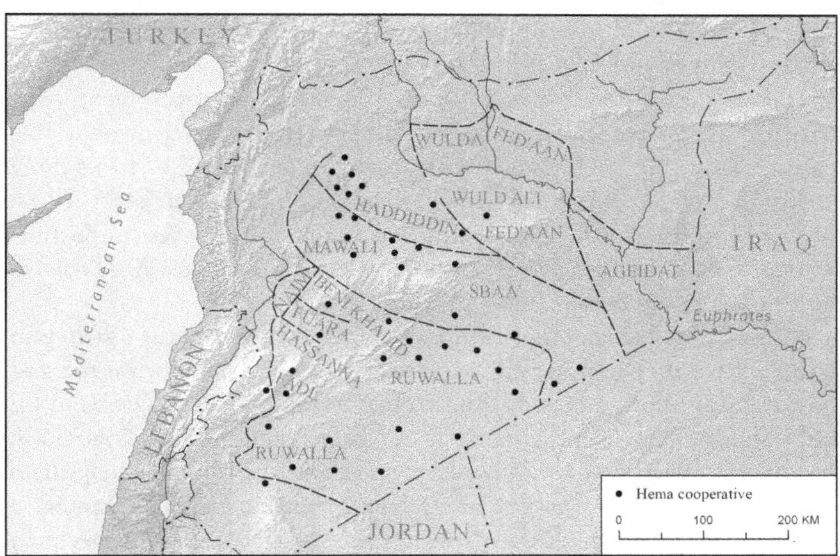

Map 6. *Hema* cooperatives and tribal areas

Nevertheless, the more powerful 'noble' tribes were not generally members of these cooperatives. Once sheep raising had become widespread, the distinction between 'noble' and 'common' tribes became blurred. Here, with the government sponsored *hema* system, was an opportunity for the 'noble' Bedouin to re-establish the traditional distinction between 'common' client tribes and 'noble' patron ones. *Hema* cooperatives, therefore, were made up mainly of client tribal groups (such as the Mawali, Wuld Ali, Haddiddiin, and some Al-Hassanna). Members of patron tribes (such as the Al-Ruwalla, Sbaa', Amarat, and Fed'aan) simply did not join these cooperatives.

A number of other factors also need to be considered. First, the 'noble' Aneza confederation still maintains strong ties with sections of their tribes in Saudi Arabia. When the Syrian Agrarian reforms in the late 1950s and early 1960s were enacted, it was the 'noble' tribes (particularly the sheikhly families) that were most profoundly affected. Among the Ruwalla and the Fed'aan, government confiscation of large tracts of their land resulted in large-scale immigration to Saudi Arabia. Members of these tribes turned Saudi Arabia into their base of operations, maintaining Syria as a satellite range.

Second, large subsidies are given to the sheikhly households of each of the Aneza tribes by the Saudi family. A program providing every Bedouin with an annual stipend of approximately U.S. $15 per head of livestock is also run by the Saudi family. The generally better-off 'noble' Bedouin tribes are able to raise their livestock in Saudi Arabia without government inference and use the range in Syria for part of the year as a source of additional pasture. Over the past few years, these tribes have come to focus more attention on a secondary activity – movement of goods between borders. It is these 'noble' Bedouin tribes who are coming to specialize in the same sort of activity that has proved so profitable to Al-Fadl and Al-Hassanna households in the Bekaa Valley.

In Saudi Arabia, programs to settle the Bedouin and turn them into farmers have slowly given way to projects designed to improve the vast range lands of the country. Factors such as the rising internal demand for meat and the rapid deterioration of the steppe land have contributed to making the government gravely concerned about the country's range land resources. By 1977, the success of a few experimental stations encouraged the government to support the expansion of *hema* as a grazing-management system throughout the country. In addition, the Saudi Arabian government undertook to:

1. reconstruct from the remnants of traditional 'soil and conservation works' a widely distributed water-spreading system;
2. set up a system of feed reserves and storage facilities to assist the Bedouin;
3. develop a sheep-fattening station that would be integrated and coordinated with the feed-distribution program, thus relieving the pressure of grazing on the range land.

The Bedouin in Jordan have not escaped the impact of modernization and its effect any more than have the Bedouin in Syria and Saudi Arabia. The rural, agricultural-based segment of the ecological trilogy in Jordan is gravitating to the larger cities of Jordan and other urban centres in the Arab world. Thus the Bedouin are losing a key partner in the traditional symbiosis of the region.

Nevertheless, the continued existence of a pastoral Bedouin community in Jordan is vital, given the fact that a large part of the fresh meat consumed in the country is provided by Bedouin herders and landowners. This economic activity is particularly important because the arid and semi-arid land that defines most of Jordan can be used effectively only by the Bedouin. In this respect, the Jordanian government has recognized that there is no easy substitute for the Bedouin and their contribution to the economy of contemporary Jordan. The government is concerned with encouraging the Bedouin to maintain, if not expand, the productive capacity in which they have traditionally excelled in a terrain in which no one can replace them. From recent studies and from conversations with the present inhabitants of the steppe region, it is evident that the quality of the pastures has been declining over the last fifteen to twenty years as a result of overgrazing and poor management of the grasslands.

In the past, the pattern of land ownership in Jordan was quite straightforward, with each tribal group laying claim to one or more widely scattered areas within which they had traditional grazing rights. Yet in recent years there has been a shift to patterns of private ownership, resulting in the truncation of some of the larger pasture lands. A survey recently conducted by the University of Jordan revealed that approximately three-quarters of the

Bedouin households sampled owned land in relatively small lots of between fifty and five hundred donums. The size of these holdings was inadequate for raising even small numbers of livestock without the extensive production or import of fodder. The Bedouin participants in the survey clearly revealed their understanding of the economic crisis before them and recognized their need to revive their livestock holdings, if it was to remain their primary way of life. The government is now considering the one recommendation of the survey. If the Bedouin in Jordan, who have traditionally excelled in the art of animal husbandry, are to continue in the vocation for which they are best suited, then a planned program of man/land use must be devised. The *hema* system developed and recently implemented in Syria and Saudi Arabia could, without difficulty, be carried out in Jordan as well in the near future.

THE ECOLOGICAL TRILOGY

The past one hundred fifty years in Northern Arabia have been especially turbulent. Bedouin tribes, after migrating north and west from the *Nejd* into the *Badia*, enjoyed a period of expansion along the borders of cultivation. This period was characterized by a particular relationship with the agriculturalists. Not being entirely self-sufficient, these Bedouin required subsidiary sources of agricultural income in order to be viable. This requirement was traditionally obtained by trade or domination over the agricultural population. The hold over the settled communities during this period of expansion took the form of *ghazu* or *khuwa*.

After 1850, when the competition between tribes for pasture and water rights had subsided, *khuwa*, or 'tribute of brotherhood', became widespread. This form of dominance was only the other face of the raiding relationship. By abstaining from raids and protecting a community from the raids of others, pastoral units collected protective tribute, usually in the form of agricultural products. On the one hand, agricultural settlements safeguarded themselves against raids by paying a 'tribute of brotherhood' to the Bedouin. And, on the other hand, the pastoral communities provided themselves with alternative solutions, besides trade, to their basic need for agricultural goods.

These tribute relationships between pastoralists and agriculturalists could only exist in the absence of strong central government, as was the case throughout most of the 1800s. With the military efforts of the late

Ottoman Empire and the European penetration during the early 1900s, the relationship of pastoral dominance over agricultural communities grew weaker. The superior military technology of the late Ottoman Empire effectively reversed the raid-tribute relationship in some areas and re-imposed the collection of government taxes. With the French military efforts of the mandate, pacification of cultivated areas and later the *Badia* became almost complete, and *khuwa* and *ghazu* were officially though not effectively restricted. The ability of the Bedouin to dominate the agricultural settlements was greatly reduced, and an important source of subsidiary income, raiding or collecting tribute, was lost. Not only were the pastoralists' means of insuring access to agricultural products curtailed, but the social distinction between *khuwa*-paying sheep raising tribes, and *khuwa*-collecting camel raising tribes began to blur. The weaker tribes had once paid *khuwa* to the stronger ones. Thus 'common' sheep raising tribes frequently paid tribute to the 'noble' camel raising tribes. This relationship between tribes continued until the mid-twentieth century. One example is the *khuwa* payments made to Abdul Aziz of Saudi Arabia by all the tribes who recognized his superior strength. Later, with the discovery of oil, he reversed the relationship and began to give generous stipends instead to these tribes.

Perhaps the most far-reaching development during the French Interwar Mandate was the establishment of a national infrastructure. Originally intended as an aid to military control over the region, the system of roads began by the French was to affect dramatically the pastoralists' total organization. Camels, as the major economic wealth of many pastoralists, were rendered increasingly obsolete as new systems of transportation became operative. Furthermore, the Bedouin found themselves easily accessible to national authorities, and some tribes, therefore, began to return to their original pre-expansion frontiers. Those Bedouin remaining in areas under mandate control attempted to adapt to their new environment. In some cases, government subsidies to tribal leaders substituted for *khuwa* payments (from the mandate power to the Bedouin tribe). In general, however, the viability of the pastoral economy depended upon the development of new channels of access to agricultural products. The improved network of roads permitted a greater degree of trade. And French authorities also reported increased trade relations between pastoralists and sedentary communities – with the roadways serving as long marketplaces.

The mandatory policy vis-a-vis the Bedouin provided another alternative in the search for access to agricultural produce. As land in the *Badia* and on the borders of cultivation came to be registered in the names of tribal leaders, access to crop production was ensured. Some land was rented to tenant farmers in exchange for a portion of the agricultural harvest. Other areas were seasonally cultivated by the Bedouin themselves. In an effort to provide themselves with supplementary income, the Bedouin increasingly turned to trading, farming, and renting of agricultural lands. This trend was further accelerated by the technological development in the region. By the early 1960s, truck transport was adopted by both 'common' and 'noble' Bedouin tribes to mobilize further their way of life in the face of the rapidly changing environment of the Middle East.

In some respects, the term 'ecological trilogy' has been employed as though it were peculiar to Middle Eastern society. The concept of three mutually dependent, ecologically based types of communities – the city, the village, and the pastoral camp – has for decades dominated the way the cultures of the Middle East are perceived. Each of these communities is seen as contributing to the well-being of the other two sectors of the trilogy and thereby to its own well-being. As a diagram, the relations in the ecological trilogy are often represented as follows:

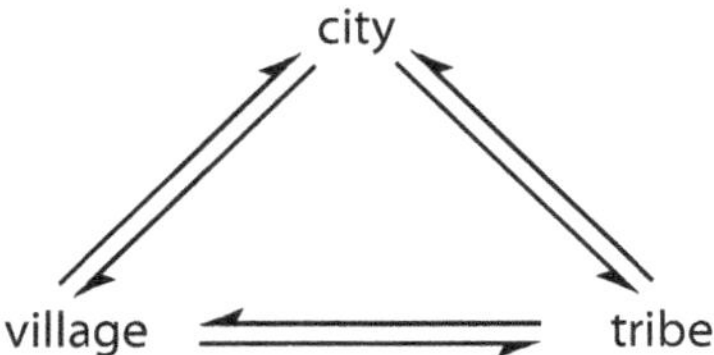

Given the dramatic changes in the region over the past decades, to what extent is this relationship still peculiar to the Middle East? Is it not more an expression of a universal aspect of social life, the need of any community for external relations? The fragmented nature of the habitable environments in the Middle East, with large stretches of barren or inhospitable land separating areas compatible to human habitation, has perhaps exaggerated that aspect of social existence that demands outside relations. Just as 'no man is an island', no community exists in a vacuum, but is tied in relations of interdependence with other communities. In the Middle East, the highly mobile pastoral populations have more dramatically carried out a role of connectors between their own communities and others.

Given the transformation of the Middle East over the last fifty years, to what extent does the city-village-tribe relationship continue to exist? Today, the Bedouin are found in cities, villages, and the semi-arid steppe land. They cross all three sectors of this trilogy and are part of the three different niches. The one common factor that remains is that whether actually raising livestock in the steppe land, fattening sheep in agricultural regions near market centres, or distributing pastoral products in urban centres, their economy is oriented towards livestock production. Perhaps an 'economic trilogy' composed of three mutually dependent specialized sectors would come closer to encompassing the total meaning of the ecological trilogy in the Middle East today.

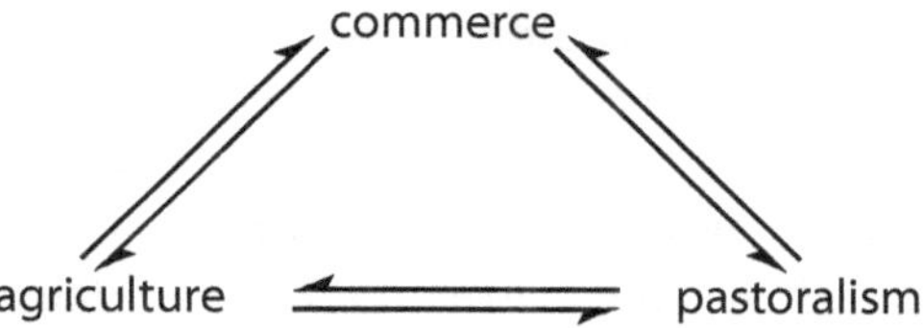

This is not simply a matter of relabelling a traditional relationship. Rather, in the light of new factors such as the truck and the pervasiveness of mechanized transport, the ecological trilogy can be better understood as relating to the broad economic system of the Middle East. The widespread changes in the region over the past few decades only highlight the distinguishing aspect of the ecological trilogy. It is the interdependence of three occupational specializations, not the types of residence patterns, that must be stressed.

MODERNIZATION OR SETTLEMENT

Since independence, many difficulties have arisen between pastoralists and central authorities. While the French Mandate authorities were content to permit and encourage the Bedouin to maintain a separate identity (Rapport, 1927), the independent nation-state was not. The situation of a 'state within a state' has been deemed inimical to the ideal of national unity. Predictably, these difficulties between the tribal political system and modern central governments have been veiled in an economic idiom by government officials. Consequently, the settlement and transformation of pastoralists into cultivators has been urged, not for political integration, but for the economic integration and advancement of a marginal and primitive people.

Today the Bedouin are effecting their own widespread integration into the regional economy without a major restructuring of their society. It was not necessary, as many had believed, for the pastoralists to settle and become cultivators in order to modernize and become integrated into the regional economy. The process of adaptation, whereby this integration was made possible, reveals the fundamental importance of livestock for these pastoral populations. It is livestock that holds a dominant place in their system of values. This attachment is not necessarily to a particular form of livestock. When the camel raising Bedouin in the *Badia* found their herds were no longer marketable, they did not give up their way of life and become cultivators. Rather, they found that, by incorporating the truck into their way of life, sheep herding could be effectively undertaken instead. Another example of the emotional attachment to the herd is evidenced by traditionally sheep raising pastoralists in marginal areas of cultivation. Even though they have begun to diversify their economic activities, their ultimate aim is still pastoralism. Their hope is to accumulate sufficient capital to buy land, which can be used primarily for pasture, not for cultivation. Furthermore, though many of the Bedouin are adopting increasingly sedentary residences and diversifying their economy, their ultimate aim remains the raising of livestock.

The decades-old debate as to whether pastoralists can modernize or must inevitably give up their way of life and settle down as agriculturalists or unskilled labourers still takes place among government officials and academicians alike. Furthermore, the appearance of permanent structures among pastoralist communities is always taken as a sign of the degeneration or decay of a way of life. It is as though the traditional pastoral life is regarded as a static or unchangeable system, except in a negative fashion. The intrusion of Western elements is too often selectively viewed as the first step in the destruction of a way of life. In Northern Arabia, the spread of permanent housing among pastoralists is viewed as a sign of the decay of their way of life. The appearance of Western or 'modern' technology in rural agricultural areas, however, is not associated with the degeneration of the traditional rural community. On the contrary, the appearance of tractors instead of wood ploughs, of cement-block houses in place of the traditional and ecologically better adapted dried-mud houses, is viewed as a sign of the modernization or development of the rural countryside.

Up to the present time, no effort had been made to look more deeply into the issue of change in Bedouin life. What appears as a form of settlement is simply an adaptation made possible by the greater mobility of truck transport. Pastoral communities can now afford to keep permanent structures, while at the same time integrating themselves as livestock specialists into the regional market system. Stone houses are built in areas where the communities spend the greater portion of the year. These units are only abandoned during the seasons of the year that require the herds to be moved to distant pastures not within easy reach of the settlement, even with truck transport. In a broad sense, the truck in Bedouin communities, the tractor in agricultural settlements, and the automobile in urban areas are all symbolic of the general transformation (or modernization) of life in Northern Arabia.

Among the Bedouin, as in communities throughout the Middle East, Western items are replacing traditional ones with breathtaking speed. Gas stoves are coming to replace wood and camel-dung fires, textiles imported from Japan and England are rapidly replacing local cloth, village-made tent sidings are gaining acceptance over those woven by Bedouin women themelves, Thermos bottles are finding their way to the tent *majlis* in place of the traditional coffee beakers. Radios, tape recorders, cameras, Chinese porcelain handleless cups and Bulgarian teapots are all becoming common household items. To bemoan the passing of traditional ways is misplaced sentimentalism. Not to recognize these changes as indicators of the close relations and interdependence of all sectors of Middle East society is to refuse to acknowledge the pervasiveness of the increased mechanization of the twentieth-century world.

As for the camel, its demise may prove to be the most important factor in returning to the Bedouin a local respectability commensurate with their expanding economic contribution to the region. For decades, if not centuries, the Bedouin have been stereotyped as part of the baggage of the camel. This association has been to the detriment of the Bedouin and has contributed significantly to the negative attitude towards them by the majority of Arab officials and bureaucrats. Camels, as Richard Bulliet tersely points out,

> are regarded as humorous animals or alternatively as stupid and nasty ones ... Fortunately camels are immune to the demoralizing effects of slander. Less happy is the situation of the Arab people who have been plagued by the irrational identification in the Western mind of them with this allegedly ridiculous beast. Most educated Arabs of today have little or no knowledge of camels or even less association with them. The insistence of Westerners upon considering them to be only hours removed from the camel herd is at best a bad joke and at worst an embarrassment. Because the camel is derisively regarded by the West, it has come to be regarded by many Arabs as a symbol of backwardness (1975: 217–218).

As the Bedouin come to be associated less with the ancient camel and more with the modern truck, there is hope that the cultural gap that separates this population from the rest of Middle Eastern society will eventually be bridged.

The future of the Bedouin and their contribution to the regional economy remains to be seen. The universe of the individual Bedouin is no longer the *Badia* or the desert fringe, but the whole of the Middle East and the international market nations. As a population, however, much depends upon the question of political integration. Thus far, pastoral groups, though integrated into the regional economy, have yet to achieve political integration into the nation-state. This issue is a double-edged sword. On one side, central authorities, recalling the anarchic activities of the Bedouin prior to independence, are trying to settle them and turn them into controllable cultivators. On the other side, the Bedouin, fearing enforced settlement, often refuse to register themselves as citizens, and thus they deny themselves a voice in government.

Appendix A. Glossary

a'gaal. A headband made of camel's hair, holding the hatta or kufiya in place.

ahl-il-beit. Mistress of the home.

'aqiid. Leader, commander.

asil. Noble, pure origin.

ashiira. Sub-tribe.

Badia. Semi-arid steppeland west of the Euphrates River.

beit. House, tent, family.

Beit. Minimal lineage.

beit hajjar. Stone house.

beit sha'ir. Cloth house, tent.

bint amm. Female first cousin (daughter of the uncle).

dhimmi. 'Protected people,' Christians and Jews tolerated by Islam in Moslem-ruled territory.

diya. Blood-money, vengeance payment.

Eid-il-adha. Feast of Immolation or Greater Bairam, marking the end of the Pilgrimage.

fakhad. Maximal lineage or branch of a tribe.

ghazu. Raid.

hajj. Annual pilgrimage to Mecca required of every Moslem once in his life if possible.

harah. Residential quarter or area.

hatta. Head cloth worn by men, also called *kufiya.*

hijra.	The flight of Mohammed from Mecca to Medina; the year it occurred, 622, is the base year of the Moslem era.
hema.	Protected range or pasture land.
ibn amm.	Male first cousin (son of the uncle).
ikhwan.	Brotherhood; adherent of the Wahhabi movement.
ird.	Female honour, modesty, prudence, chastity.
jala.	Expulsion.
jezireh.	Semi-arid steppe land east of the Euphrates River.
khamsa.	Group of closely related male agnates, generally holding some collective duties and responsibilities.
khayaal.	Horseman, generally a young man.
khuwa.	Tribute of brotherhood.
kishk.	Sun-dried mixture of yoghurt and cracked wheat.
laban.	Yoghurt.
maal-al-badal.	Monetary assistance for the annual pilgrimage to Mecca.
mahr.	Bride wealth.
majlis.	Sitting area, reception room, men's session.
mandiil.	Headcloth worn by women.
mangal.	Brazier where Arabic coffee is generally prepared.
mansaf.	Traditional dish of whole lamb served on a large tray with bread, rice, or cracked wheat.
maslakh.	Slaughterhouse district.
mawali.	Dependent client people or tribe.
mukhtar.	Village or town mayor or leader.
nargili.	Water-tobacco pipe.

nawwar. Gypsies; itinerant traders and tinkers found throughout the Mediterranean Rim.

qabila. Tribe.

qanat. Underground water system.

raa'i. Sheep herder, generally a young boy.

radwah. Token presentation to gain consent, agreement (to release a first cousin for marriage).

sharaf. Honour.

sharif. Descendant of Hasan, grandson of Mohammed the Prophet.

shawaya. Sheep raisers, 'common' tribes.

solh. Peace making, reconciliation.

sunna. Custom associated with Mohammed the Prophet.

thoub. A full-length robe worn by men and women.

tibn. Straw.

tifl. Sugar-beet pulp.

wali. Legal guardian of a minor, a woman or of one incapacitated.

wastah. Intermediary, mediator.

Appendix B. Table of Measures

Donum.	1/10 of 1 hectare
Hectare.	2.47 acres
Kilometre.	0.62 mile

Selected Bibliography

Abou-Zeid, A. 'Honour and Shame among the Bedouin of Egypt', *Honour and Shame,* ed. J. Peristiany, University of Chicago Press, 1966.

— 'The Changing World of the Nomads', *Contributions to Mediterranean Sociology,* ed. J. Peristiany, The Hague: Mouton, 1968.

Abu-Jaber, K. *et al. The Bedouin of Jordan: A People in Transition.* Amman: Royal Scientific Society, 1978.

Akkad, H. 'The Nomad Problem and the Implementation of a Nomadic Settlement Scheme in Saudi Arabia', *Land Policy in the Near East,* F.A.O., 1967.

Al-Faour, F. *Social Structure of a Bedouin Tribe in the Syria-Lebanon Region.* Ph.D. dissertation, University of London, 1968.

Asad, T. *The Kababish Arabs.* London: C. Hurst and Co., 1970.

Ashkenazi, T. *Tribus Semi-Nomades de la Palestine du Nord.* Paris: Librairie Orientaliste Paul Geuthner, 1938.

— 'The Anazah Tribes', *South Western Journal of Anthropology* **4**: 222–237, 1948.

Awad, M. 'Settlement of Nomads and Semi-Nomadic Groups in the Middle East', *International Labor Review,* 1959.

— 'Nomadism in the Arab Lands of the Middle East', *Problems of the Arid Zone,* UNESCO, No. 18, 1962.

— 'Living Conditions of Nomadic, Semi-Nomadic, and Settled Tribal Groups', *Readings in Arab Middle Eastern Societies and Cultures,* eds. A. Lutfiyya and C. Churchill. The Hague: Mouton, 1970.

Barth, F. 'Father's Brother's Marriage in Kurdistan', *South Western Journal of Anthropology* **10**: 164–172, 1954.

— 'Land Use Patterns of Migratory Tribes of South Persia', *Norsk Geografisk Tiddsskrift Bind* **XXII**: 1–11, 1960.

— 'Nomadism in the Mountain and Plateau Areas of S.W.Asia', *UNESCO Proceedings,* 1962.

— 'Capital, Investment and Social Structure of a Pastoral Nomad Group in South Persia', *Capital, Savings and Credit in Peasant Societies,* eds. R. Firth and B. Yamey, 1964.

— 'Competition and Symbiosis in North East Baluchistan', *Folk,* 15–22, 1964.

— *Nomads of South Persia: The Basseri Tribe of the Khamseh Confederacy.* New York: Humanities Press, 1964.

— 'Economic Spheres in Darfur', *Themes in Economic Anthropology,* ed. R. Firth, 1967.

— 'On the Study of Social Change', *American Anthropologist* **67**: 661–9, 1967.

Basha, O. 'Problems of Nomads in Syria', *Proceedings of the Arab League* (in Arabic), 479–484, 1965.

Bell, G. *Syria, the Desert and the Sown.* London: W. Hernman, 1907.

Bonnenfont, P. 'L'évolution de la vie Bedouine en Arabie Centrale', *Revue de Occident et de la Mediterranée Musalmane,* 1977.

Boucheman, A. de. 'La sédentarisation du désert de Syrie', *Asie Française,* 140–143, 1934.

Bulleit, R. *The Camel and the Wheel.* Cambridge, Mass.: Harvard University Press, 1975.

Burckhart, J. *Travels in Syria and the Holy Land.* London: John Murray, 1822.

— *Notes on the Bedouin and the Wahabys.* London: Henry Colburn and Bently (1967 reprint), 1831.

Capot-Rey, R. 'The Present State of Nomadism in the Sahara', *UNESCO Symposium,* Paris, 1962.

Caskel, W. 'The Bedouinization of Arabia', *Studies in Islamic Cultural History,* ed. von Grunebaum. American Anthropological Association Memoir No. 76, 1954.

Charles, S.J.H. 'La sédentarisation entre Euphrate et Balik', *Note d'ethno-sociologue,* Beirut, 1942.

Cole, D. *The Social and Economic Structure of the Al-Murrah: A Saudi Arabian Bedouin Tribe.* Ph.D. dissertation, University of California, Berkeley, 1971.

Coon, C. *Caravans: The Story of the Middle East.* New York: Henry Holt, 1965.

Cunnison, I. *Baggara Arabs.* Oxford: Clarendon Press, 1966.

— 'Nomads and the 1960's', Inaugural lecture, University of Hull, 1967.

Dalton, G. (ed.). *Economic Development and Social Change.* Garden City, New York: Natural History Press, 1971.

Dalton, W. 'Economic Change and Political Continuity in a Saharan Oasis Community', *Man* **8**: 266–283, 1969.

Dickson, H. *The Arab of the Desert.* London: George Allen and Unwin, 1949.

Doughty, C. *Travel in Arabia Deserta.* London: Jonathan Cape Ltd., 1888.

Draz, O. *Report on the Development of Rangeland and Fodder Production in Saudia Arabia.* Rome: F.A.O., 1977.

— *Role of Range Management: The Campaign against Desertification.* UNDP Regional Office for West Asia, 1977.

Dyson-Hudson, N. 'Factors Inhibiting Change in an African Pastoral Society: The Karimojong', *Black Africa,* ed. J. Middleton, 1970.

— 'The Study of Nomads.' *Journal of Asian and African Studies* 7: 1–27, 1972.

English, P. 'Urbanities, Peasants, and Nomads: The Middle East Trilogy', *Journal of Geography,* 1964.

— *City and Village in Iran: Settlement and Economy in the Kerman Basin.* Madison, Wisconsin: University of Wisconsin Press, 1966.

— 'Origin and Spread of Qanats in the Old World', *Proceedings of the American Philosophical Society* **112**: 170–181, 1968.

Epstein, S. 'Economic Development and Social Change in South India', *Economic Development and Social Change,* ed. G. Dalton. Garden City, New York: Natural History Press, 1971.

Evans-Pritchard, E.E. *The Nuer.* London: Oxford University Press, 1940.

— *The Sanusi of Cyrenaica.* Oxford: Clarendon Press, 1949.

— *The Position of Women in Primitive Societies and Other Essays in Social Anthropology.* London: Faber and Faber, 1965.

F.A.O. *Land Policy in the Near East.* Rome (compiled by Mohammed Riad El-Ghonomy), 1965.

— *Near East Regional Study: Animal Husbandry Production and Health, Fodder Production and Range Management.* Rome, 1972.

— *F.A.O. Expert Consultation on the Settlement of Nomads in Africa and the Near East.* Cairo, 1972.

Fernea, R. *Shaykh and Effendi: Changing Patterns of Authority among the El-Shabana of Southern Iraq.* Cambridge, Mass.: Harvard University Press, 1970.

Firth, R. *Essays on Social Organization and Values.* London: Athlone Press, 1964.

— (ed.) *Themes in Economic Anthropology.* London: Travistock Publication, 1967.

Firth, R. and Yamey, B. (eds.) *Capital, Savings and Credit in Peasant Societies.* London: George Allen and Unwin Ltd., 1964.

Fisher, W. *The Middle East: A Physical, Social and Regional Geography.* London: Methuen Press, 1971.

Ford Foundation. *Sheep Production in the Middle East and North Africa.* Beirut, 1971.

— *Cooperative Sheep and Forage Project.* Beirut, 1972.

Forde, C.D. 'The Habitat and Economy of the North Arabian Badawin', *Geography* **18**: 205–219, 1933.

— 'Ecology and Social Structure', *Huxley Memorial Lecture.* Royal Anthropological Inst., 1970.

Gellner, E. *The Role and Organization of a Berber Zawiya.* Ph.D. dissertion, University of London, 1958.

Gerholm, T. *Market, Mosque and Mafraj: Social Inequality in a Yemeni Town.* Stockholm: Stockholm Studies in Social Anthropology, 1977.

Glubb, J. 'The Economic Situation of the Transjordan Tribes', *Journal of the Royal Central Asian Society* **XXV**: 448–459, 1938.

— *Handbook of the Nomads, Semi-Nomads, Semi-Sedentary Tribes of Syria.* G.S.I. Headquarters, 9th Army, 1942.

Goody, J. (ed.) *The Developmental Cycle in Domestic Groups.* Cambridge: Cambridge University Press, 1971.

Grant, C. *The Syrian Desert.* London: A.C. Black, 1938.

A Handbook of Arabia 1. London: Her Majesty's Stationer's Office, 1917.

Helms, C.M. *The Cohesion of Saudi Arabia.* London: Croom Helm, 1981.

Horton, A. *A Syrian Village in Its Changing Environment.* Ph.D. Dissertation, Harvard University, 1961.

Hourani, A. *Syria and Lebanon.* London: Oxford University Press, 1946.

Ibn Khaldun. *The Muqqadimah.* Translated by F. Rosenthal. New York: Pantheon Books, 1958.

Irons, W. 'Livestock Raiding among Pastoralists: An Adaptive Interpretation, *Papers of the Michigan Academy of Science* **50**: 393–414, 1965.

— *The Yormut: A Study of Kinship in a Pastoral Society.* Ph.D. Dissertation, University of Michigan, 1970.

Irons, W. and Neville Dyson-Hudson (eds.) 'Perspective on Nomadism', *Journal of Asian and African Studies* 1972.

Issawi, C. *The Economic History of the Middle East.* Chicago: University of Chicago Press, 1966.

Johnson, D. *The Nature of Nomadism: A Comparative Study of Pastoral Migrations in S.W. Asia and North Africa.* Chicago: University of Chicago Press, 1969.

Kaberry, P. *Women of the Grasslands.* London: Her Majesty's Stationer's Office, 1952.

Kuper, H. 'Costume and Identity', *Comparative Studies in Society and History* **15**: 348–367, 1973.

Lattimore, O. 'Inner Asian Frontiers of China', *American Geographical Society*, 1951.

Lewis, B. *The Arabs in History.* London: Hutchinson's University Library, 1956.

Lewis, I.M. *A Pastoral Democracy.* London: Oxford University Press, 1961.

— *Social Anthropology in Perspective.* New York: Penguin Books, 1976.

Lewis, N. 'The Frontiers of Settlement in Syria 1800–1950', *International Affairs* **31**: 48–60, 1955.

Longrigg, S. *Syria and Lebanon Under French Mandate.* London: Oxford University Press, 1958.

Mansfield, P. *The Arabs.* London: Allen Lane, 1976.

Marx, E. *Bedouin of the Negev.* Manchester: Manchester University Press, 1967.

Miksell, M. 'Notes on the dispersal of the Dromedary', *South Western Journal of Anthropology* **11**: 231–245, 1965.

Montagne, R. *La Civilisation du Désert.* Paris: Hachette, 1947.

Muller, V. *En Syrie avec Les Bedouins.* Paris: Librairie Ernest Leroux, 1931.

Musil, A. *Manners and Customs of the Rwala Bedouins.* American Geographical Society, 1928.

Nelson, C. (ed.) *The Desert and the Sown: Nomads in the Wider Society.* Institute of International Studies, Research Series No. 21, Berkeley: University of California, 1973.

Nicolaisen, J. 'Political systems of the pastoral Tuareg in Air and Ahaggar', *Folk* **1**: 67–131, 1959.

— *Ecology and Culture of the Pastoral Tuareg with particular reference to the Tuareg of the Ahaggar and Air.* Copenhagen: National Museum, 1963.

— 'Ecological and historical features: A case study from the Ahaggar Tuareg', *Folk* **6**, 1964.

Nutting, A. *The Arabs.* London: Hollis and Carter, 1964.

Obermeyer, G. *Structure and Authority in A Bedouin Tribe: The Aishaibat of the Western Desert of Egypt.* Ph.D. Dissertation, University of Indiana, 1969.

On Indigenous and Tribal Populations. I.L.O. Geneva, 1962.

Oppenheim, M. *Die Beduinen,* Vol. 1. Leipzig: Otto Harrassowitz, 1939.

Paine, R. 'Lappish Decisions, Partnership, Information Management, and Sanctions: A Nomadic Pastoral Adaptation', *Ethnology* 52–67, 1971.

Peristany, J. (ed.) *Honour and Shame: The Values of Mediterranean Society.* Chicago: University of Chicago Press, 1966.

Peters, E. 'The Proliferation of Segments in the Lineage of the Bedouin of Cyrenaica', *Journal of the Royal Anthropological Institute* **90**, 1960.

— 'Some Structural Aspects of the Feud among the Camel Herding Bedouin of Cyrenaica', *Africa* **37**, 1967.

Rafiq, A.K. *The Province of Damascus: 1723–1783.* Beirut: Khayat, 1966.

Randolph, R. *The Social Structure of the Qdiiraat Bedouin.* Ph.D. Dissertation. University of California at Berkeley, 1963.

Rapport sur la situation de la Syrie et du Liban soumis au conseil de la Société des Nations. Ministère des Affaires Etrangères, France, 1923–1938 (14 vols.).

Raswan, C. 'Tribal Areas and Migration Lines of the Northern Arabian Bedouin', *Geographical Review* 494–504, 1930.

— *Black Tents of Arabia.* New York: Creative Age Press, 1947.

Raynaud et Martinet. *Les Bedouins de la Mouvance de Damas.* Beirut: Contrôle Bedouin, 1922.

Report on Fodder Development Project in the Hermel District. Office of Animal Production, Beirut, Lebanon, 1972.

Report on Milk and Milk Product Consumption: Problems and Solutions. Compiled by Dr. Oulaby, Beirut, Lebanon, 1973.

Sahlins, M. 'The Segmentary Lineage: An Organization of Predatory Expansion', *Comparative Political Systems*, eds. Middleton and Cohen, 1967.

— 'Tribal Economics', *Economic Development and Social Change*, ed. G. Dalton. Garden City, New York: Natural History Press, 1971.

Salisbury, R. *From Stone to Steel.* London: Cambridge University Press, 1962.

Salzman, P. 'The Study of "Complex Society" in the Middle East: A Review Essay', *International Journal of Middle East Studies* **9**: 539–557, 1978.

Schneider, H. 'Pakot Resistance to Change', *Continuity and Change in African Cultures*, eds. Bascom and Herskovits, 1959.

Sharp, L. 'Steel Axes for Stone Age Australians', *Human Organization* Summer, 17–22, 1952.

Spicer, E. *Human Problems in Technological Change: A Case Book.* New York: Russell Sage Fdn, 1952.

Stenning, D. 'Transhumance, Migratory Drift, Migration Patterns of Nomadic pastoralism', *Journal of the Royal Anthropological Institute* **87**, 1957.

— *Savannah Nomads.* London: Oxford University Press, 1959.

— 'Household Viability among the Pastoral Fulani', *The Developmental Cycle in Domestic Groups*, ed. J. Goody. Cambridge: Cambridge University Press, 1971.

Sweet, L. (ed.) *Peoples and Cultures of Middle East: An Anthropological Reader.* Garden City, New York: Natural History Press, 1970.

Swidler, W. 'Adaptive Processes Regulating Nomad/Sedentary Interaction in the Middle East', Paper for Nomad Symposium, Cairo, 1972.

Tribus Arabes de Syrie. *Haut Commissariat de la Republique Francaise en Syrie et au Liban.* Service des Renseigenments. Sections d'Etudes. Beirut, 1922.

UNESCO. *A History of Land Use in Arid Regions.* Arid Zone Research No. 17, 1961.

— *Problems of the Arid Zone.* Proceedings of the Paris Symposium, 1962.

— *Nomades el Nomadisme au Sahara.* Arid Zone Research No. 19, 1963.

UNESOB. 'Nomadic Populations in Selected Countries in the Middle East', *Studies in Selected Countries in the Middle East.* Beirut, 1970.

Volney, (Constantin-Francois Cassebeuf). *Voyage en Egypte et en Syrie.* La Haye: Mouton, 1787.

Warriner, D. *Land and Poverty in the Middle East.* London: Oxford University Press, 1959.

— *Land Reform and Development in the Middle East.* London: Oxford University Press, 1962.

Westermarck, E. *The History of Human Marriage.* New York: Allerton Book Co., 1922.

Weulerrse, J. *Paysans de Syrie et du Proche-Orient.* Paris: Gallimard, 1946.

Yacoub, S. *Sociological Evaluation of a Pilot Project for Bedouin Settlement: A Case Study.* U.N.E.S.O.B. Beirut, 1969.

— *Sedentarization of the Nomadic Populations in the Countries of the UNESOB region.* U.N.E.S.O.B. Beirut, 1970.

— *A Socio-Economic Survey of the Settler-Candidates in the Qatrana Irrigated Farming Pilot Project in the East Jordan.* U.N.E.S.O.B. Beirut, 1972.

Index

A

Abdul Aziz Al-Saud 20, 47, 48, 51, 55
Abdullah (King) 50–1
Abu Ali 3, 93–4, 96–8, 100–04, 106, 110–13, 116, 123, 128, 134, 136–7,
adaptation 10, 22, 26–8, 43, 92, 139, 152–3
Aden 45
Adra 85
aerial bombings 57
a'gaal (headband) 90
aggression 71, 102
agricultural 5, 13, 17, 23, 24, 26, 29–32, 35, 40–1, 43, 53, 59–60, 69, 90, 103, 110, 112, 116, 119, 126, 127, 128, 131, 134, 135, 139, 143, 147–53
  harvest, transport of 106, 115
  land, registering 85
  products, payment for 115
Ahl-il-beit (mistress) 112, 121
'akhi (my brother) 68
Aleppo 17, 28, 34, 38–41, 48, 52, 54, 59, 64, 130
Alexandretta 52
Alliances 44, 79, 82, 84
'ammi (my uncle) 64, 68
Amarat 38–9, 56, 146
Aneza [tribe] 8, 25, 36–40, 50, 53, 55–7, 60, 74, 79, 81–2, 84, 140, 146
animal husbandry – *see* livestock, raising of
Anglicans 46
Anti-Lebanon Mountains 3, 88, 96, 104, 120, 137
apical ancestor 37
'aqiid (leader) 138
Arab 3, 5, 7, 16, 18–21, 33–7, 42, 45–8, 52, 57, 62, 64–5, 67–71, 82, 153–4
  Society 26–7, 61–89,
Arabia 5, 6, 31, 45, 48
  Central 32–3, 42, 47, 48, 53, 55–6, 60, 75
  Northern 5, 17–18, 20, 22, 24–5, 28, 32–5, 36, 42–3, 44–60, 61, 64, 72–3, 75–7, 90, 94, 118, 130, 138–9, 142, 143, 148, 152–3
Arabian
  Caravan route 32–3, 37–8
  Peninsula 25, 32
  Plateau 28–32, 35, 141
arms 40, 45, 52, 54, 56–7
ashairi (tribal) 7
ashira (kinship organization)
Aswad-il-Tasha [wells] 141
assimilation 12, 133–4
Authorities, British 50–1
  French 5, 52–4, 58, 73n, 75–5, 149, 151
  Lebanese 88
  Ottoman 38, 42, 74
  state 13, 77, 86, 149, 151, 154
  tribal 59
authority 4, 5, 6, 8, 11, 13, 24–6, 30–1, 33–8, 40, 43, 47, 50–1, 53–5, 57–8, 60, 62, 73, 77–84, 86, 89, 98
  basis of 80, 82, 84
  moral 4, 13, 73, 87

B

Baalbek 34, 137
backwardness 1, 21, 46, 49, 130, 139, 154
Badia (arid and semi-arid steppe of Northern Arabia) 5, 11, 17, 19–2-, 24, 26–30, 35–41, 43–4, 49–53, 56, 58, 60, 70–1, 74–7, 76, 79, 81–2, 114, 120, 129, 138, 140–2, 145, 148–50, 152, 154
Baghdad 17, 34, 38–9, 52, 64, 82
Bahrain 57

Index

barley 120, 128, 132, 145
Barth, Fredrik 21, 133–5
Basra 45, 48
Bedouin
  Ageidat 54–5
  -ness 6, 8
  economy 10, 13, 27, 32, 73, 90n, 126, 130, 135, 139, 147, 149, 151–2, 154
  'common' Bedouin 7, 24, 31, 35, 37, 43, 140, 146, 149–50, 157
  nation of Bedouin tribes 72, 76,
  'noble' Bedouin 7, 19, 24, 28, 31, 35, 36, 37, 43, 141, 145–6, 149, 150
  non-Bedouin origin 4, 33, 83
bedu–hadar dichotomy 5
bedu ruhhal (migratory / travelling) 7
behaviour norms 20, 61, 70
beit 63, 91–2, 104, 108, 159
  Abu Ali 93–4, 134
  Abu Mohammed 93
  hajjar (house of stone) 91–2
  sha'ir (house of hair) 91–2
Beit 63, 73–4, 76–86, 94–6, 98, 100, 103, 126–7, 136–7, 159
  Beit Faour 73, 78, 82–3
  Beit Ibn Milhem 73, 79–80
  inter-*Beit* disputes 77
  Beit Kaakaa' 79
  Beit Saalih 94–6, 101, 109
  Beit Sha'laan 73, 78–9, 81, 85
Bell, Gertrude 40–1
Bekaa Valley 1, 3, 13, 37, 74, 80, 82, 84, 87–8, 91, 107, 114, 116, 120, 135, 146
Benedictines 46
benign neglect 3–4, 138
Beni Khalid [tribe] 55, 82
Beni Rashid [tribe] 41
Beni Sakher [tribe] 141
bidoon (without) 9
bint amm 64, 98, 155 (female first cousin)
birth 100–01
'blood money' 97, 155
blood-ties 64
bride wealth 64, 98, 156
bran 120
British 9, 45, 47–50, 56–7, 75
  Authorities – see Authorities, British
  Corridor 75
  -mandated territories 20, 26, 42–3, 51, 56–7, 75
butcher 135
butter 107, 121, 123, 128
  sheep milk 114–15
  sale of 114–15, 123
  traditional transactions 123

C

camel 7, 17–19, 23–4, 30–2, 35–7, 43, 53, 60, 92, 102–4, 108, 110, 115, 118, 128, 138, 140, 146, 149, 152–4
  baggage 22, 27, 106, 107, 114, 120
  decline in market for 140
  obsolescence of 22, 102–4, 107
  renting of 106–7, 126
campsites 107, 110, 128, 140
'Capitulations' 44
Capuchins 46
Car 2, 73–4
Carmelites 46
carrying capacity 116, 133
cash 115, 121
Catholic 46, 53
  charity (French) 46
  missionary work 49
change 8, 10, 13, 20, 21, 26, 39, 43, 44, 54, 59, 65, 69, 74, 76, 78–9, 88–9, 127, 138–9, 150–1, 153
  resistance to 1, 21, 139
cheese 107, 145
  factory, 142
  making 103, 107
Chtaura 87, 123
Cilicia, cession of 53
Circassians 40, 64, 75, 86
citizenship 3–4, 9
coffee 2, 92, 121
  brazier (*mangal*) 92, 156

Index

collective territory 11
colonial era 11
communication system 58
community consciousness 20
Conference of 1925 55
corporate interests, basic 73, 76–7, 89
council of elders 73, 77, 96, 98
cousins 7, 62, 64, 96, 98, 100, 109, 110, 136, 137
  paternal 100
cousin-marriage – *see* marriage 64, 100
credit 121, 130, 145,
crops 23, 29, 30, 115, 127, 134
  production of 29, 134
  harvesting of 9, 23, 114, 127, 129
cultivation 9, 22–4, 26, 31, 40, 43, 59–60, 107, 140, 145, 150, 152
  rain-fed 22–3

D

Damascus 2, 4, 7, 17, 19, 34–8, 41–2, 52, 53, 55, 64, 77, 78, 81, 82, 84–6, 130,
dairy products – *see* cheese, milk, yoghurt
death 66, 100
Deir-ez-Zor 40, 54–5
desertification 12
dhimmi ('Christian and Jewish protected peoples') 44
disputes 96
  arbitration of 11, 73, 82
  settling internal 76, 79,
diya (vengeance) group 97–8
'divide and rule' 51, 60
divorce 65–6, 110
Dominicans 46
dress (*thoub*) 90–1, 157
drivers 142
drought 24, 30, 34, 36, 116, 143
Druze [people] *see also* Jebel Druze 40, 52–4, 63–4, 67, 75, 86
Druze Revolt 54

E

economic 8, 12, 17, 25–6, 32, 40, 43–6, 51, 57, 60, 62–5, 69, 74–5, 86–8, 111, 136–40, 147–8, 151–3
  change 44, 65, 127
  development 20, 138
  power / strength 8, 26, 32, 45, 58, 86–7, 136
  pursuits / activities 26, 37, 104, 127, 133, 135, 138, 153
  rationality 1–2
  wealth 87, 149
education, formal 110–11
Eid-il-Adha [feast] 131, 155
elopement 101
enterprise, commerical and transport 133, 136
entrepreneurship 14, 59, 132, 134
equal social level 88
ethnic group / ethnicity 5–9, 61, 70
Euphrates 32, 35–8, 48, 50, 59, 141–2, 155
'evil eye' 104
expulsion (*Jala*) 77, 156

F

Faour, Emir 1–3, 54, 73, 77, 79, 82–3, 87
Fadl, Al [tribe] 1–2, 35–8, 41–2, 54–5, 59–60, 63, 65, 66, 73–5, 77–9, 82–3, 86–9, 93, 97–9, 102, 108–9, 114–16, 123, 127, 132–6, 146
Fadl, Sheikh 1–2, 73, 82, 84, 90, 104, 106, 115–16, 126
fakhad (maximal lineage) 73–4, 76–7, 96–8, 155
family 8, 14, 25, 26, 47, 48, 61–4, 66–71, 79–80, 82, 85–7, 92–4, 96, 113, 119, 120, 121, 123, 126, 136–7, 142, 146
  expenditure 116
  extended 1–3, 63, 68
  honour 70
Farhan-il-Meshhour 55, 77
Faware (al-Fadl) 55

Index

Faysal, King 42, 50–1
Feasts 87, 109, 110, 116, 127, 132
Fed'aan, Al [tribe] 1, 23, 25, 37, 38, 43, 53, 55, 58–60, 94, 97, 113, 115, 118, 119, 122, 124–5, 129, 141, 146
Fertile Crescent 32
fertilizing fields 114
feuds, intertribal 75–6
fodder 144, 148
Franciscans 46
four-wheel drive vehicles – see motor vehicles
French
  Authorities 5, 52–4, 58, 73n, 75–5, 149, 151
  -mandated territories 3, 9, 20, 26, 42–3, 50, 51–6, 58–60, 75–7, 81, 149, 151
frontier zone 30, 40, 50, 74
funerals 116

G

de Gaulle, General 85
genealogical tree 95, 100
generosity, traditional value of 4, 8, 14, 20, 71, 79, 85, 87–9
ghazu (raids) 35, 35, 39, 44, 54, 58, 137–8, 148–9, 155
girls 91, 101, 108, 110, 119, 127, 128
Glubb, J. 85
goat 18, 22, 30, 69, 88, 92, 106, 114, 118, 121, 134
Golan, The 37–8, 41, 45, 82, 86
grain, production of 59, 144–5
'grass roots' 80
graze / grazing 3, 5, 7, 9, 12, 18, 21, 22, 24. 27, 36–7, 59, 60, 72, 107, 114, 120, 126, 129, 141, 146–7
  access to 140
  pattern of 114
  uncontrolled / overgrazing 12, 142–4, 146

H

hajj (pilgrimage) 132, 155
Hama 34, 36–7, 39–40, 54–5, 59, 75, 79, 84
harvest – *see* crops
Hassanna, Al [tribe] 1, 8, 14, 37–40, 42–3, 53–4, 59–60, 68, 71, 73–4, 87–80, 84–7, 89, 91, 96, 98, 102, 114, 116, 118, 120–1, 123, 126–7, 131–4, 146
hatta (head cloth) 90, 155
Hauran, The 39–40, 54, 74, 86
headband (*a'gaal*) 90, 155
head cloth (*hatta*) 90, 155
hema (Bedouin system of range management) 144–6, 148, 156
hema cooperatives 144, 146,
herds 7, 10, 12, 13, 22, 24, 27, 31, 60, 69, 84, 106, 110, 114, 119–20, 127–30, 132–6, 139–42, 152–3
  depletion of 129, 133–5
Hijaz, The 33, 38, 42, 48, 50, 56
Himyar, The 32
Homs 34–8, 40, 54, 59, 64, 75, 78–9, 84–5. 87, 108, 114, 130
honour 33, 69–70, 83, 85, 87, 156, 157
horsemen (*khayaal*) 106
hospitality 4, 8, 14, 18, 20, 69–71, 85, 87
hostility 55, 69–71
household chores 112–13
Howeitat [people] 57, 140
Husein (grandson of Mohammed the Prophet) 47

I

ibn amm (son of father's brother) 64, 98, 156
Ibn Khaldun 41, 57
Ikhwan, the [warriors] 48, 56–7, 75, 156
India 45, 49
individualism, growth of 26
infrastructure, national 20, 58, 60, 149
inheritance 66–7, 85
interstate activity 137–8

Index

Inter War Mandate 3, 25, 42, 59, 138, 149
investment 87
  capital 116, 134,
ird (female honour) 69–70, 156
irrationality 1, 21, 154
irrigation system (*qanats*) 55, 144, 157
Islamic Caliphate 19, 33

J

Jala (expulsion) 77, 156
Jebel Al-Nasariyyah 52
Jebel Druze 40, 52–3
Jed'aan ibn Muheid 41
Jesuits 46
Jezireh (arid steppe land east of the Euphrates River) 37, 59, 156

K

karam (hospitality) 4, 14
kerosene 116, 124
khayaal (horsemen) 106
khamsa unit of male relatives 63–4, 67, 97–8
khuwa (tribute) 23, 30, 35, 39, 55, 148–9, 156
kidnapping 97, 101
Kinda [tribe] 32
kin group 8–10, 13, 62–4, 67, 69–70, 73, 92, 96
kinship 7, 9, 62–3, 67–8, 72, 90n, 96, 135, 138–9
King-Crane Commission 42
kishk (*laban* prepared with cracked wheat) 123, 127, 156
knowledge 154
  indigenous 12
  traditional 12, 37
Koran 33, 47, 65, 67, 98, 110
Kuneitra [district] 78
Kurds 34, 63, 64, 67, 75, 86
Al-Kuwatly [Syrian President] 85

L

laban (yoghurt) 123, 127, 156
labourers 139, 142, 152
labour expenditure 121
land
  degradation 11–12
  desire to acquire 128
  holding / ownership 11, 58–9, 67, 84–5, 96, 133–4, 147–8
  range 21, 129, 140, 142–7
  rental payments 23, 60, 84, 86
  reform 13, 20, 84–6, 89, 144, 146
  rights 11, 13, 59, 74–6, 86, 144, 147
  state owned 11, 107
  unregistered 59
  use 11–12, 74, 76, 96, 128, 143, 147–8, 152
landlord–tenant relationship 88
Latakia 52
law, customary (*urf*) 11
Lazarists 46
leadership 4, 11, 13, 26, 32, 33, 34, 37, 47, 55, 67, 74, 78n, 79, 82, 84, 87, 88, 89, 136, 138, 145
  traditional 79, 87, 88, 89, 136, 145
League of Nations 49
Lebanon 1–4, 7–9, 13–14, 0, 50, 52–3, 65, 91
'line through open desert' 50
lineage
  maximal 73, 96, 155
  minimal 63, 73, 94, 96–8, 109, 155
  organization 6, 26
  tribal 3, 4, 11, 13, 26, 37,
  segmentary 6, 8, 10, 13
livelihood 5, 7, 9, 10, 12–13
  strategies 10, 12–13
livestock
  herding of 5, 6, 7, 9, 13, 130–1, 133, 152
  raising of 5, 7, 18, 22, 27, 42, 60, 118, 130–1, 133–4, 138, 140–1, 143, 146, 148, 151–2
loyalty 20, 61–2, 70, 87,
loyalties, traditional 85

M

maal-al-badal (monetary assistance for pilgrimage to Mecca) 38, 156
mahr (bride wealth) 64–6, 156
majlis (meeting or sitting area) 3, 4, 82, 92, 102, 112, 136–7, 153, 156
male agnates 74, 136–7, 156
Mamluks 34
mandiil (scarves) 90–1, 156
mangal (brazier for coffee) 92, 156
maqtoumeen (silenced) 9
market 10, 27, 38, 106, 113, 119, 121, 126, 127, 130–2, 135–8, 140–1, 143, 151, 153
  demands 130, 135
  for milk 123
  world 126, 154
marketing 121, 130, 133–4, 138, 140
  of livestock 118
marriage 64–6, 70, 79, 98, 100, 101–2, 109–10, 116
  alliances 82
  of cousins 65, 98, 100,
maslakh (slaughterhouse) 135–6, 156
Mawali tribes 33, 35–7, 40–1, 53–5, 76, 82, 146, 156
Maysoun [poet] 19
meat, demand for 134, 143, 146
Mecca 17, 19, 32–3, 36, 38, 47–8, 50, 155, 156
Mechanics 142
medical facilities 142
medicine 116
Mediterranean coastline 28, 30, 34–6, 45–6, 49–50, 60, 64, 74
Méhariste (French camel corps) 53–4, 76
Mesalikh [tribe] 79
Mesopotamia 31, 33, 45, 50
migration 7, 24, 29, 35, 40, 53, 54, 60, 103, 106, 120
  reduced 107, 110, 121
  routes 9, 13, 114, 116, 121
  seasonal 50, 60, 74, 79, 106–7
  tribal 75
migratory cycle, annual 120
milk 24, 103, 114, 118–19, 120–1, 123, 128, 140
  milking 68–9, 103, 113, 118, 120–1
  picking up by dairy trucks 104
'misconduct' (of women) 70
mobility 10, 13, 22, 24, 26, 31, 58, 72, 77, 79, 84, 87, 108, 118, 133, 135, 140, 142, 153
  upward 133–4
  downward 133–4
modernizing 139–40
Mohammed (the Prophet) 19, 33, 47, 82, 156
moral system 89
'mosaic' of cultures 61
motor vehicles – *see also* transport, mechanized; trucks 10, 13, 58, 79, 83, 120
Mu'awiyya, Caliph 19
Muqaddimah [book] 41
Mutton 135

N

Napoleon 45
nargili (water-pipe) 101, 110, 156
national rule 25
nation-state 4, 5, 21, 27, 51, 77, 78, 89, 151, 154
  era 11
  modern 11
Nefud, the 28
Neighbourhood 63, 67–9
Nejd, the 53, 75, 79, 148
Nomad 5–7, 21, 28, 133
  'problem' 21
nomadic pastoralists – *see* pastoralists
Nuri Sha'laan [Emir of Ruwalla Tribe] 42, 54, 58, 77, 81, 82 85

O

oasis 5, 23, 28, 32
orchards 103, 128
Ottoman 20, 25, 35, 36, 38–42, 44–9, 51–3, 59, 73n, 81–2, 86, 149
  rule 25, 41–2

Index

overgrazing – *see* grazing

P

pastoralism 7, 20–22, 24–6, 27, 30, 34, 36, 41, 86, 138–40, 151–2
  cyclical nature of 25, 30
  diversification of activities in 27, 138, 152
  nomadic 6, 18, 29–30, 34, 56
production in 138
pastoralists 1, 11, 21, 22–4, 27, 30, 31, 57, 114, 130, 139, 143, 148–9, 151–2
  pastoralist–middleman relationship 123, 130, 136
  nomadic 5–6, 12
  semi-nomadic 5
  semi-settled 5
  settled 5, 152
pasture – *see also* graze 7, 9–11, 17, 23, 28–30, 34, 37–9, 50, 54, 56, 58, 60, 73–6, 78–9, 84–7, 92, 106, 114–16, 118–20, 128–9, 133, 135, 140, 142–3, 145–8, 152–3
  allotting of 73
  rental fees for 115
  seeding of 120, 128–9
patrilateral 63, 67
payments, voluntary 84, 88
Persian 32–3
  Gulf 28, 45, 48–50
Pilgrimage 33, 38, 155–6
ploughing 143–5
  of marginal areas 143
  prohibition of 145
politeness 70–1
polygamy 65
potential fighting force 81
power 7, 31, 32, 35, 36, 38, 40–2, 44, 46, 47, 50, 51, 53, 58, 73, 75–7, 78, 84, 149
  economic 8, 58, 86–8
  political 56, 86
  military 26
  moral 13, 87
Presbyterians 46
presentations, voluntary – *see* payments, voluntary
private ownership, patterns of 147
private sphere / world 67–9
property 54, 64, 66–7, 74, 133–4
  communal 74, 84–5
  rights 75
    lack of 144
puberty 101
public sphere / world 67–8

Q

Al-Qaa caves 120
qabila (tribal organization) 7, 63, 73–4, 76, 96
qanats (irrigation system) 55, 144, 157
qayd il-dars (under study) 4, 9
Qurayish [tribe] 33, 39, 83–4

R

raa'i (sheep-herder) 106
races, of motorcycles and cars 110
radwah payment 98, 157
raids (*ghazu*) 35, 35, 39, 44, 54, 58, 137–8, 148–9, 155
'ranching' 133–4
range management (*hema*), Bedouin system of 144–6, 148, 156
range usufruct 142, 144
Raqqa 141–2
refugees (Armenian, Kurdish, Assyrian and Catholic) 34, 51, 53
resources 8, 11, 21, 30, 45, 59, 87, 104, 135, 137, 140, 143, 146
  misuse of 144
resilience 10
responsibility, moral 88
rivalry 46, 48, 70–1
Al-Riyadh 47
roads 20, 58, 103, 106, 138, 149
  network 60, 127, 149
Royal Air Force 57
Rub'al-Khali, the 28

rugs, making / weaving of 103, 107, 121
Russia, Czarist 46
Al-Ruwalla 40, 53–5, 58, 60, 73–4, 77–9, 81–2, 85–7, 89, 146

S

Sab'a Biyar [*qanat* system] 114
Salamiyeh 40, 78, 84, 87
sales 121, 123, 131, 135
commercial 121
Sattam Sha'laan 40
Saudi Arabia 4, 6, 12, 14, 17, 25, 27, 43, 47, 51, 64, 77–9, 81–2, 85, 87, 140–1, 143, 146–7
Saud, King 85
Sbaa' [tribe] 38–40, 53, 55, 60, 74–5, 79, 84, 146,
scarves (*mandiil*) 90–1, 156
school 46, 52, 55, 69, 142, 145
seasonal
  cultivation 150
  labour 7, 60, 108–9, 126–7, 132, 134–5
  migration – *see* migration, seasonal
  pastoral cycle 120
sedentary communities, relations with 22, 30, 77, 127, 134, 139, 149
sedentarization 11, 133–5
Seljuks 34
semi-feudal 86
shame 69
Shammar
  Bedouin [tribe] 8, 25, 36–9, 53, 55–7, 59, 140
  Confederation 8, 55, 140
Sharaf (honour) 69–70
Sharif (descendant of grandson of Mohamed) 47, 50, 157
Sheep 7, 18, 22, 24, 26, 27, 30, 31, 35–8, 40, 43, 60, 68–9, 87, 88, 92, 102–3, 106–7, 111, 114–15, 118–21, 126, 128, 130–2, 134–8, 140–7, 149, 151–2
  clipping of 126
  commercialization of raising 27
  distribution of 130–2, 135–7,
  fattening (station) 142, 144, 147
  herders (*raa'i*) 106
  market 27, 38, 119, 121, 126, 130–8, 140–1, 143, 149, 151
  nomadic husbandry of 18, 143
  sale of 'unwanted lambs' 131–2
  slaughter of 132, 135
  stratified pattern of production 138
sheikhs, 'assembly' of 55
shepherds 13, 106, 120, 132–3, 136
singing 110
slaughterhouse (*maslakh*) 135–6, 156
social services 142
solidarity 7
  family 62, 67
  female 103
  political 76, 89
  tribal 11, 33–4, 77
specialization, of occupations 130, 151
state–tribal interaction 3
steppe land 9–12, 17, 31, 33–4, 47, 59, 114, 138, 143–7, 151
stone houses (*beit hajjar*) 3, 85, 91–2, 96, 129, 136, 142, 153, 155
storage facilities 147
students 142
subsidies 55, 146, 149
subsistence 13–14, 37, 130
Suez 45, 49, 50
sugar 116, 118, 121
  beet (pulp – *tifl*)107, 120, 127, 129, 134, 157
supplies, general 106, 121, 142
suspicion 50, 71
sustainable practices
Suweida 41
Sykes-Picot Agreement 49
Syria 1–8, 11–12, 14, 17, 20, 23, 25, 27, 31–2, 43, 48, 50–3, 58, 78, 81, 85–6, 94, 118, 119, 137, 141, 143–8

T

Tabqa 142
Tamir el Milhelm, Emir 1

Index

tea 110, 116, 118, 121, 122, 124,
technology, advancement in and adoption of 10, 13, 26, 32, 44, 73, 140, 150, 152
telegraph network 58
telephone 142
tent, white 80, 126
thoub (long dress) 90–1, 157
tibn (alfalfa) 120, 157
tifl (sugar beet pulp) 120, 129, 157
Trad, Sheikh 42, 59
trade 4, 7, 13, 30, 32–3, 38, 45, 50, 68, 104, 123, 127, 148–9
tragedy of the commons theory 11
transnational relations 4
transport, mechanized 20, 22, 151
Trappists 46
Treaty of Sèvres 53
Treaty of Al-Muhammara 75
tribal 7, 9, 20, 23–4, 26–7, 33–4, 36, 41, 47, 50, 51, 53, 54–6, 58, 60, 63–4, 66, 69, 73–8, 86, 89, 94, 96, 100, 102, 128, 130, 133, 137, 140–1, 144–7, 150–1
  affiliation 62, 90
  council 73, 77, 82, 84, 96
  elders 3, 11, 73, 77, 86, 88, 96–7, 104, 130
  feuds / disputes 11, 38–40, 43, 55, 71, 75–6
  leaders 4, 8, 13–14, 54–6, 59, 76–8, 85, 87–8, 142, 149
  lineage – *see* lineage, tribal
  marginal tribal society 24
  territory / property 11, 50–1, 59, 62, 74–76, 84–6, 143
    seizure of 142
  units 24, 63–4, 74, 76, 88, 94, 96–7, 104, 128, 130, 133, 137, 140, 145
tribes – *see also* individual tribe names
  'common' 7, 24, 31, 35, 37, 43, 140, 146, 149–50, 157
  'noble' 7, 19, 24, 28, 31, 35, 36, 37, 43, 141, 145–6, 149, 150
  pastoral – *see also* pastoralists 19–20, 30–1, 50, 65
  sub-tribe (*ashiira*) 73, 96, 155
tribute (*khuwa*) 23, 30, 35, 39, 55, 148–9, 156
  tribute-raid relationship 23
trucks 10, 22, 26–7, 43, 60, 102–11, 114, 116–17, 118–39, 140–3, 150–4
  ambiguous advantages of 143
Turkman 63, 64, 86

U

Umayyad dynasty 19
Um Ali 94, 100–2, 112, 113
Unitarian reform movement – *see* Wahhabi reform movement
urban brokers 131
urban merchants 44, 121
urf (customary law) 11
usufruct 142, 144
utensils 22, 92, 110, 113, 116

V

values, basic 138–9
vegetables 120
veiling 70
vengeance unit – *see also khamsa* 64, 97, 102
vetch 120, 128, 132
visiting / visitors 3–4, 68, 79, 82, 84, 87–8, 92, 100–1, 104, 108–10, 112–13, 119, 120, 129

W

Wahhabi reform movement 36, 47
Wastah (intermediary) 67, 157
Water 10, 11, 27–9, 31, 37, 39, 56, 60, 96, 110, 118, 127, 140–2, 147–8
  camions / trucks 60, 140
  pipe (*nargili*) 101, 110, 156
  resources 11, 140
wealth 32, 41, 64, 77–8 85–9, 94, 98, 106, 130, 132–3, 149
wheeled vehicles 32

wood, for fires 143
women 3, 65–70, 90–2, 100, 110–10, 112, 114, 118–23, 127, 142, 145, 153
  daily work of 68–9, 91, 110–12, 118,
  older 92, 110,
  unmarried 108
wool 19, 24, 114, 115, 128
  brokers 126
  merchants 114, 121
  production 123, 126
World War I 20, 26, 47–9, 75
woven crafts 104, 153
Wuld Ali [tribe] 38–9, 41, 74, 146
Wuld Sliman [tribe] 55

Y

yoghurt (*laban*) 123, 127, 156
'Young Turk' Revolution (1908) 46

www.ingramcontent.com/pod-product-compliance
Lightning Source LLC
Chambersburg PA
CBHW021818270326
41932CB00007B/233

* 9 7 8 1 8 7 4 2 6 7 7 2 0 *